INSTINCTUAL RACISM

& OUR PRIMAL TENDENCIES

AN EXPLORATION OF OUR INNATE TRIBALISTIC INCLINATIONS

ENRIQUE AVILES

For those who engage in wonderment and contemplation about the inner machinations of our human nature.

FOREWORD

I write this book as a way to make sense of what I observe around me in regards to human nature and human behavior as well as what I have observed about my own proclivities and inclinations. It's an exercise in self-reflection, observable behavior in others, and contemplation about what drives our behavior. It is through self-examination, self-reflection, and contemplation that we gain a better understanding of ourselves and the world around us. Through this process of reflection, as we gain a better insight and understanding of ourselves and our own behavior, we can then better understand others. It is an exercise in recognizing our own behavior and our human tendencies so that we can better understand from whence these derive and, in so doing, have a greater awareness of the impetus and origin of our behaviors so that we are able to better manage and become better navigators of these behaviors as we embark on our lifelong journeys of becoming the persons that we are capable of becoming.

One of the things that is an amazing aspect about being human is our capacity for continuous learning and personal growth. We have the capability, if we choose to exercise it, to learn and grow throughout our lifetimes, well into advanced age. In fact, continuous learning and engaging in new experiences is recommended for good brain health and to thwart the decline of brain function as we age. Of course, one has to be open to personal growth and development, it doesn't just occur by happenstance. One has to actively seek it and engage in it. This is often easier said than done. Sadly, many of us become set in our ways and our thought processes. So much so, that we close our minds to new forms of knowledge, new insights, new experiences, and new ideas – new ways of viewing the world – especially those that challenge our notions of what we have come to accept as "our own." We develop an attitude of comfortable complacency. We find comfort in the familiar. It's the path of least resistance and, as per our human nature, we would rather choose to take that path. For, who wants to choose the path of most resistance? A path filled with twists and turns, rocky terrain, steep inclines, and maybe even hazards along the way? Those who want to be challenged do! Those who seek growth and self-development. For, just as a muscle needs to be challenged to grow and develop, so do we as persons. Without challenges, without testing ourselves, without stepping out of the comfort zones of our minds, we plateau as persons and we fail to reach our full potential. We can also plateau as a collective group of people – as a nation in this regard.

Of course, exposure to new knowledge or new ideas is not, in and of itself, positively productive. There are some really bad ideas out there and lots of misinformation presented as viable (flat earth, really?). One has to be judicious about this process. Just like anything else, there is a risk involved in stepping out of one's comfort zone. However, that is where growth takes place.

Another amazing aspect about our humanity is our capacity for self-awareness. We are able to think about who we are as persons, our goals, aspirations, dreams, our frailties. We can contemplate about the reason for our existence and our purpose in life. We can think about the "why" of everything and search for the meaning of why things are as well as why things function the way they do. We can search for meaning. We can contemplate questions that have never been explored before. We can question answers that have already been established in the wake of new insights and new tools from which to examine them. We can also question why things are and explore new concepts and possibilities. Our capacity for such thinking is an immeasurable gift and blessing. It is indeed part of the essence of being human. As we contemplate these things, we can gain a better understanding of ourselves and the act of understanding ourselves is fundamental to understanding the world around us.

These are the exercises in which I have embarked and which have provided the impetus to share the observations thereof via this book. Some of the observations I share in this book may be difficult to read for some readers, however, I don't make them lightly or flip-pantly, but rather as an important discourse for all of us to gain a better understanding of ourselves and our primal tendencies for tribalistic behavior that manifests itself as racism and prejudice in our everyday interactions with one another. These observations are a means for us to explore and understand these tendencies within all of us.

TABLE OF CONTENTS

PART ONE:

INNATE TENDENCIES

OUR PRIMAL TENDENCIES

I like to think of myself as a generally pacific person. I consider myself to be sensitive and empathetic by nature and by nurture and may be even a bit too sensitive at times (for my own sake as well as that of my state of mind). And yet, like most of us, there have been times in my life when I have been less than sensitive. In fact, there have been times in my life when I have been outright insensitive. There have been times when I have been outright harmful towards others. This is something that I am not proud of and regret having done. Looking back as an adult to things I engaged in as a kid makes me disappointed in myself for the way I behaved and conducted myself at certain times towards others. Looking back through the critical lens of self-awareness and as a self-described empathetic person, I wish that I could have reacted better in certain circumstances and situations, that I would have exercised more compassion and empathy. I have my share of regrets and, hopefully, have learned important lessons in the process (I've often wondered how people are able claim to have lived a life with no regrets because I regret many things in my life – for things I did as well as things I did not do).

With all that being said, as pacific and gentle of nature that I consider my temperament to be, upon reflection of my overall persona, I find it interesting that I can be so readily moved to visceral excitement and uncontrollable fervor and revelry in certain situations that can be considered as gratuitous violence. Like many of us who enjoy watching sports, I find it inexplicably thrilling to witness a big hit in football or a big knockout in a boxing match or MMA fight. It's a feeling of guttural thrill and excitement that emanates from a place deep within. Something primal. I would venture to say that there is even an accompanying rush of adrenaline when this happens. Nobody taught me that these specific circumstances are thrilling, it's simply a natural reaction that I experience. And, as such, it leads me to think: where does this sort of reaction come from? Where within the deep recesses of my DNA does this seemingly automatic response stem from?

I remember going to a college football game several years ago that illustrates this point. My brother and I were sitting together high up in the stands of Arizona Stadium watching the game unfold amongst a sea of loyal fans clad in blue and red. Of course, we were raucously reveling in everything that our home town Arizona Wildcats were doing right and equally dismayed whenever they made a poor play or a "bad" officiating call was made against them. As the game unfolded, I remember a point in the game where one of "our" defensive backs laid a massive hit against a would-be receiver for the opposing team. Instantly, the crowd burst into a huge roar, myself and my brother included. I even jumped to my feet as is my tendency to do upon witnessing big plays. I quickly sat down in a cloud of shameful regret, however, upon the realization that the player that was hit seemed to be really hurt as he was not getting up. Not all fans, however, seemed as bothered by the prospect of one of the opposing players being hurt. Conceivably, because the loss of that player could turn the tide in favor of our home team and improve the chances of a Wildcat victory.

I have come to recognize that this sort of reaction is not uncommon. In fact, it seems to be the norm at sporting events. Fans revel in the misfortune of a player of the opposing team and even more so if the player is an important or key member of their squad. Some fans even wish for it. An infamous incident that further illustrates and encapsulates this phenomenon happened several years ago in Philadelphia, the city of "brotherly love." The Dallas Cowboys were in town to play the hometown Eagles in a mid-season game. Sporting events in Philly are notoriously known to be charged with ardent vitriol against opposing teams (and even against their own home teams when the Philly fans see it fit to do so), especially at football games and even more so when the opponent is in the same division (as is the case with the Cowboys), making it a very heated rivalry. As the game unfolded, there was a point in the action where the star receiver for the Dallas Cowboys, Michael Irvin, suffered an on the field injury where he was not able to get up and walk off the field to the sidelines to receive treatment. In fact, his injury was severe enough where he actually needed be taken off the field on a medical cart and then by ambulance to be transported to the hospital. Upon seeing him injured, the fans in the stadium infamously cheered at his apparent misfortune and continued to cheer when he had to be taken out of the game on a medical cart and subsequent ambulance, reveling at his misfortune. With the prospect of an imminent victory having been greatly improved because of his injury and, in addition, a hated (and talented) player being eliminated in the process, the Philly fans were feeling pretty good about themselves and their hometown team even as many in the sports media were horrified at their callous behavior caught on national television. And yet, this was not an isolated incident limited to the rabid Philly fan base. Similar reactions of varying degrees of distaste take place at almost all levels of sports – from the professional ranks, to college sports, even in high school. It's a ubiquitous enough reaction that makes one wonder about the innate machinations of human nature, namely, how we as humans can revel in the misfortune of others, especially when the "other" represents the "enemy" even when that enemy is manufactured or contrived and not actually a literal enemy intent on doing us harm. An opposing football team is not a literal invading army bent on dispensing death and destruction upon us, and, a victory by an opposing football team will not normally bring us (or our families) personal physical harm as fans, and yet, we have the capacity to conjure this notion upon them. In our mind's eye, we view them as representing a villainous enemy – one that must be vanquished and destroyed. Enough so as to wish them ill. We have the capacity to conjure the enemy but also to conjure the harm that would be committed against us by said enemy even when the potential for harm does not exist.

Sporting events are prime opportunities to bring out this kind of primal behavior in us. In the midst of the pageantry, the revelry, the sights and sounds, the crowd noise, the intense action, it is easy to get caught up in the fervor and excitement of it all and engage in behavior that lowers our inhibitions – in a healthy way, but also in a more disturbing way. In such an atmosphere, we feel free to yell, scream, cheer, and jeer. It offers us with an outlet for a form of primal expression that we don't normally have the opportunity to display in the course of our everyday lives (an emotive catharsis of sorts). And to be able to do so en masse amidst a sea of like-minded and like-spirited individuals amplifies our feeling of excitement even more so. A sort of collective energy amplifier.

This kind of behavior, however, is not limited only to sports and sporting events. It can also be fomented outside of a sporting arena. This is specifically akin to what happens nowadays at political rallies and conventions. The attendees are roused to an intensity of fervor and excitement in a sea of like-minded individuals. In such events, the collective energy mustered by such crowds creates a wave of excitement that moves and compels the participants to behave with a mob mentality of sorts similar to that of sporting events or concerts, the focus, however, not being a sporting competition but rather a political "competition." Political rallies have become a political hakah of sorts – a show of force towards the opposing side with the intent of crushing the opposition as in a football game or a rugby match. The teams in this scenario, however, are the competing political parties.

Political parties recognize the power of this approach – the "us v. them" mentality. Their intent is to motivate and mobilize their "fan" base to support the "home team" by engaging in activities that will lead the team to victory, namely through voting, canvassing, monetary donations, etc., and, in so doing, galvanize and grow the base in a way that will lead to victory at the polls. And just like a sporting event, these political events are replete with all the pageantry and revelry thereof including cheering, jeering, team colors, team logos, chants, team symbols, etc. People at these events can get roused to such a fervor that they will engage in screaming and yelling of platitudes that most attendees would not normally do outside the confines of such an event – a collectivist mentality of sorts orchestrated by a skilled conductor who is the speaker or speakers at hand and plays the audience with deftness. It is a visible show of unity, force, and power intended to send a message – essentially, the message being: "this is our team; we support our team and what it stands for and represents; our team is better than your team and if you dare challenge or oppose our team, you will be destroyed!"

THE GROUPING INSTINCT

Sporting events and political rallies are but a small sampling of the collective grouping behavior in which we all engage in some form or another as humans. We have an inner drive to group together. It is something intrinsic within us and it is also something that can be observed in nature. There is an innate drive to band together into groups that can be seen across many species of animals. It is quite common in nature and something that can be readily observed. As humans, we recognize the vast array of groupings that occur in the animal kingdom and we have incorporated into our language a way to refer to the various clusters and groups of animals that we observe. We have come to label and identify these by assigning specific names for these groupings such as: schools of fish, pods of whales, prides of lions, a flock of seagulls, herds of wildebeests, swarms of bees, colonies of ants, packs of wolves, etc. Some of these group descriptors are quite intriguing and somewhat puzzling as to their etymology and source of origin such as a murder of crows, a cuvee of quail, or a gaggle of geese. The whimsy of these labels not-withstanding, it points to the fact that, across nature, many animals have an innate compulsion to group together. It's instinctual. Again, it points to the fact that, over the course of millennia, many animals across a vast spectrum of genus and species including fish, mammals, insects, and birds have developed an instinctual drive to engage in grouping behavior as a survival mechanism. Those animals that banded together into groups had a greater chance of survival than those who didn't. As such, the grouping behavior was culled over time to what we see today across the animal kingdom in its ubiquity. It is also something that applies to us as humans as well. As humans, we also display this innate grouping behavior and, just as we have numerous ways of labeling certain groupings of animals, we have also developed a myriad of descriptors to describe the various types of groupings of people. Some of these include: group, tribe, band, posse, hoard, mob, regimen, diaspora, congregation, clan, gang, club, crew, troop, cohort, team, corps, squadron, etc. These terms speak to the numerous ways that people can band together into a group and the different purposes of those groups.

There is an innate drive to form into a group that has evolved over time and we carry this drive within us. We carry this compulsion to be part to a group. In essence, a compulsion to belong. To belong in some form or fashion to a group and, commensurately, an aversion to being ostracized and not belong. One of the greatest worries parents will have as they raise their children is for their particular child to not fit in and be accepted by his or her peers – for him or her to lack the social skills necessary to be included and to feel included and not be ostracized from the group – in essence for him or her to belong. In our adolescent years, this phenomenon takes on even greater profundity as the sense of belonging amongst our peers becomes ever more important to us as we, chronologically, draw nearer to becoming independent from our families. The familial group is gradually supplanted, in a sense, by the peer group and our peer groups become extremely important during this stage in our lives. Being ostracized during this life stage can be devastating and many a distraught young person can be susceptible to an emotional downward spiral whenever this occurs. So much so that, at times, it can lead to self-loathing, self-harm, and, sadly, even suicidal ideation. These unfortunate outcomes speak to the significance of just how important a role this phenomenon plays in our lives.

We are born into a group, that being our family, however, we expand the groups to whom we belong as we grow and develop various interests, associations, and passions over the course of our lives. We start joining groups from an early age as we embark on our educational journey and these groups expand our grouping horizons in significant ways. In addition to being part of the school itself as a baseline group, as we go through school many of us become part of a multitude of auxiliary groups as we traverse our educational journey – groups such as a sports team, a debate team, a chess club, drama club, school choir, dance, band, etc. Oftentimes, we take on the identity of these groups, our various tribes, and we become a reflection of the group itself. We do this in the way we dress (adopting a certain micro-fashion style), the way we style and wear our hair, our group lingo, and other identifiable markers that set our groups apart from other groups.

As we continue to mature and enter young adulthood, we expand our grouping horizons even more so. Some of us become part of a military group by joining the armed forces. Some of us become part of a fraternity or sorority and a myriad of other campus clubs when we go to college. When we start working, we may become part of a union or another trade or professional organization. When we have school-age children, we may become part of a parent-teacher association, a parenting group, a scout troop leader, etc. We may join a neighborhood association or other civic groups. Throughout the course of our lives, some of us join car clubs, motorcycle clubs, book clubs, knitting groups, recreational sports leagues, rotary clubs, and a myriad of other groups.

For many of us, belonging to certain groups takes on a very profound significance for us and becomes an immutable part of our overall identity and how we view ourselves (once a Marine, always a Marine; Wildcat for life, etc.). Consequently, the tribal markers that are the indicators of our affiliation to such groups also take on a great significance and we bestow upon them a lot of gravitas. We treat them with high regard and importance and proudly display these for others to see. We fly flags and banners, wear patches and emblems, we sport tattoos, stickers, decals, etc. to indicate our commitment, loyalty, and our high regard for our group associations, our tribes, as well as to indicate our tribal affiliation to them.

The groups to which we belong are an important part of who we are as a person and an important part of our identity. Oftentimes, these group associations become an inextricable part of who we are and how we view ourselves – an extension of our overall persona. These affiliations are not always readily apparent and one may not know of a person's group affiliations until that person discloses such. Other times, a person's group affiliations are very prominently displayed and well-advertised making them hard to ignore or over-look (modern-day gang culture is predicated on this premise and, as such, gang colors are worn prominently to signify one's gang affiliation).

My brother-in-law hails from New York. That is where he was raised and where a lot of his family still lives. After college, he moved away to the Southwestern region of the country, first to El Paso, Texas and then to Arizona after he met my sister. Being from New York, however, he was exposed to many things New York growing up including New York sports teams. As a kid, he was introduced to the New York Jets and he has never looked back. Today, he displays his loyalty to the Jets in a number of ways: he has tattoos that display his loyalty to the Jets, Jets jerseys, Jets decals on his vehicles, a man-cave that is teeming with Jets paraphernalia, and belongs to a Jets fan club that gathers on game-days to watch the team play (his Jets tribe). He is the epitome of a loyal fan. Regardless of the team's performance on any given Sunday or any given season, his loyalty never wavers. This is an intrinsic part of who he is and almost an automatic conditioned association that we view him through. When I think of him, it's hard to separate him from his Jets alter ego.

My brother-in-law embraces and expresses his "Jetness" in very discernable ways just as other people embrace their own partic-ular team affiliations. In our modern-day society, our sports teams, those which we claim, support, and to whom we pledge our loyalty, occupy a significant place in our lives for many of us. Sports teams are, by their very nature, extremely well-suited to meet that intrinsic need within us to be part of a group – a tribe – something greater than ourselves. And they come readily equipped with a plethora of attributes and ready-made accoutrements that meet our tribalistic tendencies including those of grouping behavior, differentiation and tribal markers, fealty, and territorialism. The fact that professional and collegiate sports is a multi-billion dollar industry is a testament to this notion. The sports industry taps masterfully into this part of our human nature – our innate tribal tendencies. When we adopt a sports team, that team becomes a very important aspect of who we are, part of our persona, our extended tribe, and we live and die by how they perform on a weekly basis and from season to season.

TRIBAL POLITICS

This sort of intense loyalty and affiliation to our teams, our tribes, however, is not limited only to our sports lives. Sports are a perfect medium to fulfill these innate tribalistic tendencies, however, the innate drive that propels and fulfills our tribalistic tendencies in a sports context also takes place in other arenas. We engage in similar behavior when it comes to the other extended tribes in our lives including our alma maters, military service, clubs, faith communities, etc. It is something intrinsic within us that drives such behavior. In this our modern society, we can see this phenomenon very clearly particularly when it comes to our political affiliations and the tribes that those affiliations represent.

Just as there are die-hard, true to the core Jets fans like my brother-in-law, there are also die-hard, true to the core Republicans, Democrats, Libertarians, Socialists, Communists, Liberals, Conservatives, etc. Whereas these political affiliations may have been regarded as important in times past, in today's divisive political climate, these affiliations have evolved to take on a much greater significance and importance for us than ever before. Today, just as with our sports teams, many of us live and die by our political party affiliations and our party's performance at election time. We also defend the tribes that these political affiliations represent against "attacks" from other tribes (the opposing parties). These, our adopted tribes, become such an important part of who we are, our identity and our persona, that we take criticisms against the party and the ideologies of the party not only as attacks on the tribe, but as personal attacks against us as individuals. We take these criticisms and attacks on the party personally as affronts to our own personal beliefs and ideologies and the values that we stand for. As such, oftentimes we react to these attacks with as much animus as if someone were attacking our own family. We resort to a fight or flight mentality wherein flight is not a viable option. On too many occasions, we have been witness to overzealously fervent political acolytes resorting to picking up arms literally and figuratively in response to such attacks. They lash out using the weapons of modern day communication as well as literal weapons in the form of firearms to defend a set of ideologies they consider to be under attack. This is what one does when one feels threatened – when one's tribe is threatened and attacked. This is what we have always done since prehistoric times. We are applying an innate compulsion that has been developed over thousands of generations to a modern-world context. And, unfortunately, it oftentimes does not yield very good results. In such a volatile socio-political climate, shouting matches and insults rarely, if ever, lead to productive discourse, compromise, and a meeting of the minds. In fact, it often produces the opposite effect whereby it provides fuel for fodder. It only incites the fire that burns within ever more and leads us to become ever-more entrenched and ossified in our beliefs, the beliefs of the party (our tribe). We rise to defend our party, our tribe, with ever more fervor and gusto – as if we were defending our own family. We tow the party line. Such is the political climate that we live in today.

This didn't just happen by chance, however, political parties have become ever more sophisticated and strategic in cultivating these intense political affiliations and very deftly leverage and utilize the modern tools of information dissemination (and disinformation) to do so. They employ the media, marketing firms, PACs, political interest groups, and individuals with influence and clout to do this.

The media and Madison Avenue recognize the importance of cultivating and fostering this tribal mentality to move us ever closer to having an intimately intense affiliation to our tribes and ever further away from the opposing tribe. It is also cultivated by a barrage of incessant rhetoric transmitted via numerous media channels, not the least of which are talk shows and talk show personalities – a continuous loop of divisive rhetoric and fodder. Our political climate has evolved into one where any semblance of civil discourse about opposing views has become an almost extinct practice and even regarded as a sign of weakness and capitulation in certain circles. Sadly, in our hyper-charged political climate of today, reaching out to find common ground or compromise with the opposing party is seen as betrayal against one's own party – a conceding of sorts of the party line.

However do we combat this? One way is to gain a better understanding of ourselves, how we develop our affiliations, and also of our own human nature, namely our inclinations and tendencies towards tribalism that is imbedded deep within us. By developing a better understanding of our intrinsic human tendencies, we can then be consciously aware that these exist within us and recognize them for what they are – basic primal tendencies. When we do that, we can then be better prepared to identify them whenever they surface and present themselves so as to modulate them as necessary. In this way, we can then be the ones in control of our primal tendencies and not let these inclinations and tendencies control us. We cannot control that which we do not recognize and what we don't understand about ourselves, for, if we are not cognizant of it, how can we expect to manage it?

Additionally, developing an awareness and an understanding of how we are being manipulated to foster these intense affiliations is another important aspect towards managing these tendencies. It is important to understand how we are being manipulated by a constant stream of hyper-divisive rhetoric from a multitude of sources (print media, radio, TV, social media, etc.) the effects of which are to make us ever more entrenched in our tribes ("tribalized") as our own party's views are touted and lauded while the opposing party's views are ridiculed and discredited while at the same time painting a picture of the opposing party as an enemy, an enemy who, because of their opposing views and ideologies, is repulsive as they threaten our way of life and, therefore, must be repressed and censured as much as possible if not altogether eradicated.

DEHUMANIZATION OF OUR FOES

As we have become ever more divided through a concerted effort of party and media strategic manipulation, we have become more entrenched in our own views and beliefs – those that align with the ideologies of the party, the party which we have come to adopt as our tribe. In doing so, we have fostered a climate of extreme suspicion towards anybody who touts and expresses something that is different or contradicts those values and beliefs that we have come to adopt as our own and which go against the party line. We come to regard such individuals who do so as enemies (not just rivals). As such, the picture that we construct of our "enemy" is painted and forged before us through this same process of circular logic via an echo chamber constructed by our media outlets. And the picture, of course, is not a pleasant one of respect and common courtesy, but rather an ugly depiction of those representing the opposing side – the "enemy." The more odious and abhorrent a picture that can be painted of the "enemy" (the opposing party), the easier it becomes to view its members as undesirable and, commensurately, the easier it becomes to treat them with a decremental regard for their inherent humanity. In essence, by vilifying and dehumanizing the members of the opposing tribe, we can then proceed with impunity to engage in behavior that infringes on their inherent humanity and inhibits their promulgation as well as the promulgation of their ideas and ideologies – a primal impulse that we have applied for millennia (an attitude of vanquishing those who oppose us and threaten our way of life in the compulsion for self-preservation of the individual and the tribe).

In our tendencies to vilify and deconstruct the inherent humanity of our enemies and present them as subhuman, I am reminded of the propaganda campaign that took place in the 1940s during World War II. As part of the U.S. war effort, through a concerted marketing campaign, both German and Japanese nationals were depicted in the most abominable way possible so as to dehumanize them and foment feelings of repulsion and anger towards them in support for the war effort at home. Posters, imagery, and war propaganda films of the time depicted Japanese and German soldiers with grotesquely exaggerated features purposely contrived so as to evoke feelings of disgust and contempt towards such "abhorrent" monsters. This is not unlike what is happening today, albeit in a more modern form, via the modern means of content dissemination and vitriolic rhetoric.

A case in point that highlights this dehumanizing tactic occurred during the last two presidential administrations, both during the Obama administration as well as the Trump administration. It was during Barak Obama's presidency that a meme was widely utilized and disseminated by his detractors in which his face was distorted to resemble that of the Joker from The Dark Knight (Heath Ledger's portrayal), done to evoke feelings of loathsomeness towards such a "villainous" individual by portraying him in a demeaning, demented, and deranged way – essentially assigning the deranged psychopathic qualities of the Joker villain to President Obama himself. Likewise, during the Trump administration, Donald Trump was depicted in a myriad of demeaning and insulting ways – from an overgrown man-baby wearing a diaper, to an orange monster-like creature on a rampage akin to the Incredible Hulk. In both of these cases the imagery that was applied to depict both presidential figures by those on the opposing side was used not only in the spirit of political satire or satirical commentary, but, rather, as a means to dehumanize them – to dehumanize them not only as sitting presidents, but as persons – to diminish and erode their inherent humanity.

One significant aspect of these dehumanizing tactics that was not present during World War II, however, is the incessant stream of information, misinformation, memes, imagery, etc. of this sort that can be disseminated and circulated via our 24 hour news cycle as well as through the ubiquity of our social media outlets, both of which can be quite addictive – more so than we like to admit or recognize. Media companies (both conventional media and social media companies alike) understand the addictive nature of this kind of content and our insatiable desire for more of it (like eating popcorn – in this case, media popcorn), their primary focus being to keep us tuned in and logged on as much as possible. As such, they do everything they can to give us more of what we crave, especially as their advertising revenue depends on it. They become, in essence, a sort of information, disinformation, and content "pusher" of sorts.

The other modern and disturbing aspect of this ubiquitous media content proliferation is that anyone can conjure misinformation and disinformation, and pass it along as valid and legitimate through a multitude of social media platforms. Social media allows for everybody to have a voice, even if that voice is based on fallacies. Along with this universality of access that social media provides comes the danger of misuse by those who have ulterior motives. Freedom of expression allows us to freely share our thoughts, opinions, and beliefs in the marketplace of ideas no matter how misguided and deranged they may be.

PART TWO:

TRIBALISTIC BEHAVIORS

AUTO-DIFFERENTIATION

Our grouping behavior evolved over millennia. It was one of the hallmarks that led to our survival as a species. We are indeed highly social creatures as a result of this. Because of this dependence and reliance on our groups for our survival, our groups, our tribes, were of immense importance to us and, commensurately, so was our standing in the group. In order for an individual to be a functional and viable member of the group, the tribe, there were certain expectations that needed to be met and upheld. Along with defending of the group against threats, being in the group and remaining in good standing with the group also meant adopting the norms of the group, essentially embracing the culture of the group in its totality (assimilating into the group).

This included adopting the particular intrinsic aspects and attributes of the group that differentiated it from other groups including group norms and customs, traditions, forms of communication, etc. It also included the visible markers – the visible identifiers – of the group, those elements that differentiated the group from other groups in the form of distinctive garb and decoration, body ornamentation, physical scarring and mutilation, piercings, tattoos, headdresses, hair style and décor, etc. Amongst the other aspects that were particular to the group, these visible tribal markers were a visually discernable way to announce to the group itself that a particular individual embraced the group in its totality and that he or she belonged to the group. It was a way for an individual to announce and affirm to the group that he or she belonged to the group (the tribe) and, commensurately, that the tribe itself accepted the individual as a member of the tribe by bestowing the group's distinctive tribal markers upon the individual, at times in ceremonial fashion, confirming and affirming an individual's membership in the tribe. In essence, the individual was claiming the tribe, but the tribe was also claiming the individual (We carry this tradition today in modern form through rites of initiation, hazing rituals, convocation, etc. when we become part of certain groups.). The adoption of unique tribal characteristics and accoutrements allowed each individual tribe to differentiate itself from other tribes. These accoutrements were also a way for other groups to visibly recognize an individual's tribal affiliation. Essentially, these tribal markers were a way for us to announce to the world which tribe we belonged to.

In our modern sports context, we wear the tribal colors of our adopted teams by way of jerseys and other team paraphernalia. In ancient times, they did not have team jerseys to wear, of course, but the tribal markers they did have were just as effectively discernable and recognizable. The distinctive nature of these differentiating traits between groups is quite evident when comparing the variety of unique customs and traditions that are specific to various Native American tribes across the Americas and how each tribe has its own unique set of traits and characteristics that they adopted as their tribal identifiers.

This innate drive to differentiate ourselves has been carried down through our ancestral lineage and can be observed by the plethora of unique characteristics displayed by the various indigenous groups today all around the globe. However, it is not limited to indigenous groups only as any one of us who belongs to a group is quick to adopt the unique norms and traits that distinguish the group from other groups and includes a wide spectrum of specific identifiers that correspond to a particular group. This behavior of needing to differentiate ourselves as a group from other groups with unique norms, customs, traditions, and markers has been carried out and handed down over millennia. I find it quite interesting that we continue this practice, albeit in more modern form, even today, including what used to be tribal body markings and body art (such as my brother-in-law's Jets tattoos).

The act of using visual cues and visible markers as a way to show our tribal affiliations is something that all of us do to some extent or another. We engage in the practice of using visible markers to show our group affiliations, to show to others that we belong to a particular group or tribe. A quick glance of the online NFL store or NASCAR store, for example, shows the myriad of ways that fans can display their tribal affiliations and their loyalties to their favorite team or driver via a multitude of merchandise choices – everything from clothing apparel to household items bearing the team logo, to decals and stickers, collectables, flags, banners, etc. Essentially, any way that a loyal fan would like to express his or her "tribal" affiliation, some sort of merchandise product exists to do just that. Some fans, like my brother-in-law, will memorialize their loyalties through tattoos of their favorite team, player, driver, etc. And, just as tribal members in ancient times applied "war" paint on their face and bodies, some modern-day fans will even engage in the practice of game day painting of their faces (and other parts of their body as well) to display their tribal team affiliation not unlike how tribes did in times past (and some continue to do so even to this day), a harkening of our tribal past in which warriors donned distinctive body paint on themselves as part of their battle preparation rituals. We can see this display of tribal marking in various contexts amongst the various groups to which we belong including our Alma Maters, military service, scouts, motorcycle clubs, gang culture, and just about any group association that we have.

I have worked in the non-profit world for the majority of my professional career and it is interesting to see how, even in the non-profit world, we engage in this practice. There have been many a community fund-raising or outreach event in which I have participated as part of my membership to a particular non-profit organization where all of us who were representing the respective non-profit organization were expected to present ourselves wearing the "team colors," team logo, team motto, etc.

Whenever we belong to a group that we have a strong connection to and strong passions for, we don the markings as well as adopt the norms and culture of that particular group to show the world our "tribal" affiliation to that particular group – just as in ancient times. We have an innate and deep propensity and compulsion for this behavior. It's quite universal and can be seen across time and across cultures around the world.

TRIBAL MARKING

My brother-in-law wears his loyalty for the Jets proudly on his sleeve for all the world to see. Everybody with whom he comes in contact recognizes quite readily his affiliation to the Jets. One can rather quickly tell that he belongs to the Jets tribe. He, and many sports fans alike, display their team affiliation in myriads of visible way via the aforementioned selection of merchandise products available. These offer a means to show one's "tribal" affiliation and where one's team loyalties lie. I find it interesting how ubiquitous these tribal markers are – across a vast myriad of contexts – and also how these tribal markers have been used over time.

When one belongs to or becomes part of a particular tribe, it is a natural behavioral response that one expresses that tribal affiliation in visible ways for others to see. We announce our tribal affiliation so that others may recognize our allegiance and discern which tribe we belong to. It is also done to indicate to the tribe itself that we are loyal to it – that we embrace our membership in the group so much so that we are willing to display our loyalty out in the open for all to see. It also announces to other tribes whereby our loyalties lie so that they may be aware of it as well.

This is something that we do throughout our lives as we expand and traverse our tribal affiliations. A very salient example of this occurs via our scholastic journey from childhood to adulthood in the context of one's alma mater as we transition from elementary school, to middle school, to high school, and then to college and beyond. At each stage, we proudly adopt the tribal markers that are representative of that school or educational institution. I experienced this first hand in my own educational journey. As I transitioned from elementary school all the way to college, I can remember first being a proud Nash Elementary Roadrunner, then a proud Amphi Junior High School Pirate, then a proud Amphi High School Panther, and ultimately a proud University of Arizona Wildcat. At each juncture, I gladly embraced the school's tribal identity and tribal markers without a second thought. I and the rest of my peers proudly sported our tribal markers in the form of school colors, school mascot, school motto, and school name that indicated our affiliation to that specific scholastic tribe. We were part of a tribe, embraced the markers of the tribe, and affirmed our affiliation to the tribe by displaying our tribal markers so that other tribes (schools) would know whereby our allegiances rested and belonged. We have a tendency to do this in a myriad of contexts to express our tribal affiliations. Motorcycle clubs have an adopted norm that exemplifies this in the way they, firstly adopt a name for their motorcycle club, develop iconography that aligns with their adopted name, and then overtly display their group's identifier via an emblem that depicts all of these elements in one distinctive design which is emblazoned on the back of their motorcycle jacket or vest that they wear while riding. It represents a visible marking tool for all to see which indicates their unique tribal identity and affiliation.

From bikers who wear their emblems on their jackets, to actual gangs sporting a specific color, to sports teams, civic groups, skin heads, goths, steam punk culture, etc., we constantly find creative ways to display our tribal affiliations. Of course, we do this with our sports teams as well. Our sports teams come ready-made for this purpose by already having a tribal name, a team logo, a team mascot, team colors, etc. and a plethora of tribal marking tools that we can purchase to announce our tribal affiliation to our respective teams. These are very important for some people and they will go to extraordinary lengths to display their tribal affiliations (I have seen custom paint jobs of a person's automobile painted with the emblem, logo, and color scheme of his/her favorite sports team). And we can observe this behavior in a myriad of other contexts where grouping behavior is involved.

For a period of time, I worked for the local branch of the nonprofit organization, United Way, conducting community development programs in Tucson, Arizona. While working there, I came to recognize how important it was for us as employees to represent the agency in a way that was uniform across all aspects of our work in the community by adopting the norms and culture of the organization. We were, in essence, members of the United Way tribe and, as such, were expected to adopt and uphold the organizational norms of the tribe in order to be functioning members of the organization. It entailed tribal markers of course. In this case, it was the "Live

United" messaging and the colors that went along with it (black lettering on a white background). There were specific rules about how this messaging was to be presented and specific expectations about how it would be displayed especially at community events. We were the United Way tribe. We "Lived United" and proudly adopted the tribal markers that were part of the United Way tribe. This was done by no sheer accident as our local United Way branch, like so many branches across the nation, received its marketing and branding directives from the national offices in very specific and explicit detail. Branding was very important to represent a unified (or in this case, "united") front. This practice of adopting organization-specific cultural norms (including tribal identifiers) is done in businesses across the country (and across the world for that matter) as company culture and cohesiveness has become an important component of employee retention and work-place satisfaction.

Branding, as we know it, is essentially tribal marking in the modern sense of the word. These visible tribal markers are quite ubiquitous and can be seen in the process of claiming one's tribal affiliations across time, across cultures, and in a myriad of contexts.

We use tribal marking to indicate our tribal affiliations, but also to differentiate ourselves from other groups. These markers serve as a way to set our own particular groups apart. Imagine if disparate groups looked the same and had the same tribal makers? Or had no tribal markers to speak of? Imagine if all sports teams used the same colors and same mascot? Or no mascot? Just generic names like Team A and Team B and a limited set of binary colors like white v. black. Tribalism and differentiation are the reasons why schools are compelled to have a mascot, school colors, school mottos, etc., and why professional teams also do the same. To do otherwise is unthinkable in our minds. That is a notion that is incomprehensible to us, and also somewhat disconcerting. We engage in this behavior because it is ingrained within us, we feel a compulsion to do so. It allows us to differentiate our tribes from other tribes and it helps our tribes to have their own particular ethos, their own specific identity. We engage in tribal marking almost as if it is second nature. As if it is imbedded within us. I contend that it is.

OUR PENCHANT
FOR DIFFERENTIATION

In the animal world, scent and the sense of smell is much more prominent a sense than for us humans. Animals utilize their sense of smell to navigate the world around them much more proficiently and effectively than we do. Their keenly adapted sense of smell allows animals to discern much about the world around them including tracking prey, avoiding predators, finding food, marking and recognizing a particular animal's territory, and discerning one pack from another. Animals are able to utilize scent to discern which group an individual animal belongs to in the same way humans use visual markers to determine the tribal affiliation of a particular person. For animals, scent is essentially their tribal marking tool and they can differentiate one another from the unique scent of each pack. Our sense of smell is not as keenly developed as that of animals. We do not rely on our sense of smell to navigate our surroundings as animals do. Nor do we use our sense of smell to differentiate tribal affiliation (for the most part). Instead, we developed other ways to differentiate ourselves from one another – tribal markers that are much more visually attuned. We can see this as we compare cultures around the world and across time and the variety of visual accoutrements and indicators that distinguish one tribe from another.

Our evolutionary origins began in ancient Mesopotamia in the Euphrates Delta region of Northern Africa. It was from whence that our earliest ancestors eventually migrated and established settlements in all habitable corners of the world. Given this common origin, it would seem that the descendants of those original peoples would carry the same tribal markers and tribal marking indicators wherever they migrated and ultimately settled. And yet, we know this is not the case. Tribes developed their own unique and distinctive tribal markers wherever they settled. A simple look at the tribal markers adopted by indigenous tribes in our own corner of the world in North America reflects this penchant for differentiation. The indigenous tribes of North America all have their own distinctive and recognizable tribal identifiers. From the Mohawk in the Northeastern US to the Seminole in the Southeast, to the Apache in the Southwestern US to the tribes of the Pacific Northwest, they all adopted their own unique tribal markers that differentiate them from one another. We, as humans, appear to have an ingrained compulsion for this behavior and one which can be seen when comparing differing groups the world over in all cultures. It is just something that we do – a behavior that is deeply ingrained in us. We are wired to differentiate our tribes from one another and wired to recognize and distinguish those differences. It is an adaptation that we see in nature amongst animals and a behavior that we, as humans, also have as it would have been necessary for survival amongst our earliest ancestors in order to maintain the cohesiveness of the tribe as well as to protect one's tribe from rival tribes.

We are wired to differentiate our tribes from one another and, as such, wired to recognize differences amongst tribes and the members of those tribes. We all engage in this behavior, consciously and subconsciously. We engage in setting our groups apart from other groups by giving our groups their own unique identity and, as such, we also engage in recognizing those differences that set other groups apart from us – the different tribal markers between groups. Consequently, we are quite observant of those markers and engage in constant discerning and recognition of the differences amongst one another. This includes intentional tribal markers such as garb and ornamentation, but also unintentional tribal markers – those inadvertent and inherent qualities that also serve as tribal markers such as skin tone, culture, language, customs, traditions, religious beliefs, political beliefs, etc. We notice when another person is different than we are as a way to discern the tribe to whom they belong. We notice if they are of different "race," a different color, have different facial features, etc. It is an autonomous response that most of the time we are not necessarily cognizant thereof as it occurs outside of the bounds of our intentional thought processes. As such, it is understandable that we notice differences. We are indeed not color-blind. In reality, we are keenly attuned to noticing differences, skin color being just one of the myriad of ways that we utilize to distinguish one another (albeit, a very distinctive one). We carry this primal proclivity that, for thousands of generations, helped our ancestors to function and survive, into a modern world where it is not necessarily applicable or practical anymore in most situations. Nevertheless, it is still there.

THE DIFFERENTIATING
INSTINCT

The act of differentiating is also the act of discriminating in the innocuous sense of the word. We engage in this all the time. A simple trip to the supermarket is replete with our constant differentiating and discriminating between products according to brand, value, size, color, flavor, etc. as we make our decisions as to which products to buy. In this context, we use our ability to discriminate in order to determine which qualities are most appealing to us and then choose the products we like best according to those preferences. Likewise, a person with discriminating taste is one for whom only certain qualities of a service or product will do. That person chooses

which product or service he or she will partake of according to his/
her preferences and standards. Differentiating is just something that
we naturally do. We apply this ability to differentiate on a regular basis
as we go about our daily activities such as which brand of orange juice
to buy…or peanut butter…or shoes, etc. Most of the time, we engage
in this behavior with relatively little turmoil or distress. This practice,
however, becomes problematic when this inherent and ingrained
behavior is applied to people. And, of course, we apply this premise
to people too. Just as our ancestors did. Our ancestors discriminated
between those groups/tribes who were friendly v. those who presented
a threat. It was eminently important that they have these abilities for
differentiation as it could mean the difference between the tribe being
over-run and ransacked by rival clans or not. It was essentially a survival mechanism in that it allowed one to recognize potential danger
and act accordingly.

In our modern society, we no longer have to be on constant
guard against rival tribes and marauding mobs looking to invade our
villages to pillage and plunder our goods as our ancient ancestors did
for millennia and, because of that, we don't need to have to the keen
differentiating instincts to recognize these invading peoples. However,
instincts don't just go away because they are no longer applicable anymore. Our instincts remain. We still carry the proclivity to recognize
and discern differences amongst others as we would an invading tribe.
Even if there isn't an invading tribe anywhere to be had. It's deeply
imbedded in us. Often, we even project the aspect of danger or threat
upon a group of people unnecessarily so – when it isn't there. We do
this in order to be in alignment with our notions and predispositions
of the perceived threat others pose to us due to their presenting differences – our perceived stereotypes of the particular group of people who possess different traits and characteristics than we do. Their

inherent differences trigger us to think that they present a danger, a threat to us, autonomously and subconsciously. We, of course, employ this notion in the context of race, color, and ethnicity. We also employ this in the context of ideological differences. The differences in ideologies between Democrats and Republicans, for example, lead us to view one another with suspicion. A suspicion that often fosters contempt akin to how we would view a rival tribe in ancient times. Blue v. red, left-leaning v. right-leaning, liberal v. conservative, Republican v. Democrat – these are signifiers of our modern-day rival tribes.

So how do we navigate and conduct ourselves in a modern world with anciently imbedded proclivities and instincts? Well, this is a question that is quite poignant and gets to the crux of the matter. In spite of ourselves, we continue to apply these proclivities just as we have for millennia, however, now we apply them in a modern world context. We continue to apply them to a modern world that does not necessarily call for such. So we find ourselves having these imbedded inclinations and proclivities that drive our behaviors without a veritable outlet to apply them. And so, we create outlets and we find ways to apply them. We do this by manufacturing our rival tribes (such as in sports) and acting accordingly against these whom we come to view as our enemies. We foment our feelings of rivalry toward those tribes whom we view as being in direct opposition to us (such as in politics, religion, climate change, gun control, etc.) and bestow upon them rival tribe status. We apply our imbedded instinctual proclivities for differentiation and use these to see the differences in others – their tribal markers that would indicate that they belong to an opposing tribe (the rival tribe). These tribal markers may be unintentional, but we see them as tribal markers nonetheless. We apply our abilities for discernment and differentiation by recognizing differences in skin color, hair, clothing, language, culture, religious practices, political ideologies, sexual orientation, and many other categories. This is a practice that is not the exclusive domain of any one group of people as it is simply human nature – all groups engage in this behavior. It is human nature imbedded within us through evolutionary biology. We are indeed not color-blind as some people claim to be (regarding race). We are, in fact, quite the opposite. We are highly attuned and discerning when it comes to color and all the other qualities that make us different from one another. We, in essence, utilize a significant portion of our senses, especially our sense of sight and hearing, as well as our mental capacities for discernment to recognize differences amongst people. We visually recognize when somebody looks different than us, dresses differently, has different customs, traditions, etc. and we also audibly discern when somebody speaks a different language, has a different accent, a different cadence, or a different volume of speaking.

Having these proclivities for discernment, differentiation, and discrimination that have been handed down to us by our ancestors does not, however, mean that we must treat those who are different from us as our enemies just because they are different – with disdain and disregard. The annals of history, however, do show how internally wired we are to do so. From the initial strifes between early rival clans, to battles between rival tribes, to battles between city-states of ancient Greece, to religious wars of the Middle Ages, to the socio-political ideological wars of modern civilization, we have always found a way to be at odds with one another over a myriad of collective differences. We have always found a way to be at odds with those whom we see as different in some way, and we base these differences on a number of factors including: physical attributes, religion, language, sexual orientation, political ideologies, economic philosophies, and more. And, as previously mentioned, when we see others as our rivals and as our enemy, we have the tendency to dehumanize them, leaving the door open for engaging in harmful and oppressive behavior towards them that denigrates and dismisses their inherent humanity. When we see others as subhuman and as threats to us and our way of life, it creates within us a mindset, a mental and moral license of sorts, whereby we can engage in acts of harm towards them with the belief that they are deserving of such harm and mistreatment due to their subhuman status that we have attributed to them. The harm inflicted could be physical harm or emotional and psychological harm, as well as institutionally-imposed harm of the systemic type.

For us, our enemies are ostensibly subhuman. If we see others as our enemies, in our eyes they are essentially lacking in inherent humanity. We see this notion played out consistently in our modern popular culture in the way that heroes and villains are portrayed whereby the heroes are typically depicted in the most positive light – visually attractive, fit, muscular, noble and representative of the highest human qualities of valor, strength, and self-sacrifice whereas the villains (the enemy) are typically portrayed with exaggerated unattractive features bordering on the grotesque with commensurate deranged, twisted minds and self-serving delusional motives where their humanity is barely recognizable, if at all (it is much easier to vanquish and destroy villains if they are monstrous and devoid of any redeemable qualities thereby eliminating any semblance of sympathy towards them) – archetypes that we have employed consistently in our literary legacy throughout the ages.

This, however, does not have to be so. Unlike other creatures, the beauty about being human is that we have the capacity for self-awareness, self-reflection, and, as such, the capacity for self-correction. When we become aware of our intrinsic inclinations and have a better understanding of the roots of these, we can engage in conscious behavior to curtail and control these tendencies. We do not have to be subject to the mercy of our internal inclinations. We can't eliminate them altogether because they are imbedded in our DNA, however, when we are aware of these, we stand a much better chance of rising above them.

AUTONOMOUS RESPONSE

Each and every one of us is the product of our experiences. Our past experiences, whether good, bad, or a combination thereof, have shaped us into the persons that we are today. We view the world through this lens. It's not always an accurate lens, but it is our lens nonetheless. However, along with our personal experiences, we are also a product of thousands of ancestral generations before us and we carry that generational legacy in our DNA as well as the instincts that helped our ancestors survive for millennia. Instincts are just that, instinctual. These are reactions and behaviors that occur in an instant without thought our contemplation. They are ingrained within us. They are autonomous responses.

Having grown up in Southern Arizona, there are many things that can prick or poke or pierce you. Almost everything has quills or thorns or spines of some sort, some more vicious than others (the quills of the jumping cholla cactus are notoriously painful!). Arizona is indeed a desert and it comes with its share of desert-dwelling creatures great and small. From an abundance of lizards to spiders to snakes, there is a plethora of critters that one can encounter simply by living in the place that they also call home, especially the further one gets away from the commotion and the hustle and bustle of the center of town. Such was the case for me. For several years, I lived away from the center of town off a winding road that used to be just two lanes before it was eventually widened (and somewhat straightened) into a four lane street. It was an area surrounded by desert terrain and several horse property owners. Living in this part of town, one would encounter desert critters on a pretty consistent basis. During the time that I lived there, I saw my share of coyotes, javelinas, bobcats, quail, roadrunners, and, of course, tons of lizards of all shapes and sizes. (I even had the unique experience of encountering Gila Monsters on a couple of occasions which are quite rare to see in the wild as their populations have decreased over time as the human population has increased). I recall one such encounter that stayed with me. As I was heading out of the house one particular morning, I stepped outside the front door onto the outer stoop that leads from the house as I normally did so many times before. However, as I was taking that last step off the front stoop, I glancingly discerned a long, tubular, brownish-greyish pattern moving alongside the bottom of the stoop. In an instant, I jumped about 4 feet off the ground and what seemed to be about 10 feet away as my momentum was such that I could not reverse course! I cleared the snake and positioned myself at a safe distance from it. The snake, however, just slithered smoothly along about its day pretty much oblivious to my frantic leap and dramatic histrionics. From the safe vantage point where I had positioned myself, I saw that it was not a rattlesnake, although the coloration was similar to a rattler. Everything happened in an instant and my heart was racing when the encounter took place as if a jolt of adrenaline had been pumped into my body. I had no time to think, I just reacted as if I was on auto-pilot mode. And, of course, I was. It was an instant and instinctual reaction to a stimulus that I perceived. Fight or flight in its purest form.

I have experienced that fight or flight sensation several times in my life, usually involving some sort of close encounter with an animal or critter (or traffic!). It is always a spontaneous reaction to something that, after the fact, could be considered harmful or dangerous such as a scorpion, spider, snake, etc. These reactions always leave me wondering about the physiological mechanisms involved to have such visceral physical and emotional responses to a perceived threat. In each encounter, I had no time to think about the situations, I just reacted – an instinctual response to a perceived threat. It is something that we all have within us and something that most of us have experienced at some point in our lives – a guttural instantaneous reaction to a perceived danger.

We have developed these instinctual responses through millions of years of evolutionary biology. They are imbedded within our limbic system of the brain – the primal, lizard brain as it is often referred. The part that processes our autonomous responses necessary for safety and survival. It is a legacy that we carry from our earliest ancestors as they navigated the world around them and came to recognize hazards in nature and reacted accordingly through fight or flight responses in order to eliminate or avoid the threat of harm and, thereby, increase their chances of survival. These instinctual responses came to be imbedded within us over millennia and were handed down over spans of generations so that we carry these same responses within us today.

In a similar fashion, we have numerous proclivities and inclinations that are encoded into our psyche that drive much of our behavior. Much of the time, we are not even aware or cognizant of these drivers and, yet, they are there such as our drive for forming into groups, our drive for tribal marking, as well as our penchant for territorialism – all stemming from imbedded tribalistic behaviors.

Given these proclivities for grouping behavior, tribal marking, differentiation, and territorialism that we carry within us from millions of years of human evolution, it is my contention that these imbedded behaviors are what drives a lot of our behavior that constitutes prejudice and racism in our modern-day society.

There are a multitude of behaviors that we engage in that stem from our primal tendencies – behaviors that correspond to our tribal ancestry. The drive to form and function as a group is one such behavior. The drive to differentiate our groups from one another is another of these behaviors. Both of these helped us to function and survive for millennia. We carry these within us still. Applying them in a modern-day context, however, is fraught with complications. In our modern society, we frown upon viewing others as different than us. This is mainly due to our having a deeper understanding of the concept of "races" and how this is a construct that we forged, and also due to our having a more evolved appreciation for the inherent humanity within each of us. These are notions that we generally accept….intellectually. However, our intellectual understandings do not always mesh with our primal drivers. Our primal tendencies are extremely powerful and they often override our intellect and empirical knowledge – as well as our good intentions.

This is evident in how we engage in grouping and differentiating behaviors even to this day and apply these as if we were living in ancient times. We group ourselves – physically and ideologically, and we react accordingly to those who fall outside the bounds of these – those who fall outside our tribal paradigms – those who, in ancient times, would have been intent on inflicting harm upon us and represented an existential threat to our tribes. In our modern day context, we react to "outsiders" as if this were still the case. We even fabricate the threat of harm meted by those groups whom we view as "outsiders" when a threat of harm does not exist. When these "outsiders" (those who are not like us physically and/or ideologically) enter our sphere, we then view them as "intruders" and engage in actions and behaviors that relay this message to them. These primal tendencies manifest themselves in the form of exclusionary practices (such as voter disenfranchisement, ownership of property, red-lining, segregation, access to higher education, etc.) and unequal access to a number of other things such as access to credit, job positions, holding public office, etc. We have a penchant for excluding those whom we view as different in some form or another.

TERRITORIALISM

nother instinctual behavior that we can observe in nature is territorialism. A wide array of animals across various species engage in this type of behavior in which they will lay claim and control over a territory as well as over other animals. Having laid claim to a specific territory, they then engage in another commensurate behavior which is that of marking their territory. This marking behavior is carried out so that other animals will recognize that a specific territory "belongs" to a specific animal or pack of animals, thereby signaling that it is under their purview and control. This is a behavior that we can see across various species of animals.

To mark their territories, animals will use urine, feces, glandular secretions, scents, vocalized sounds, etc. Once marked, in order to protect these established claims, they will engage in another instinctive behavior which is use of force and intimidation to protect and defend their territory and their pack or herd, etc. against intruders and upstart challengers. Nobody teaches animals to do this. They just do it. It is instinctive. As humans, we do this as well. We also carry this instinct to lay claim to things. We constantly engage in territorial behavior by laying claim to something and then marking of that claim. Whereas animal mark their territorial claims primarily through scents and various forms of vocalization, we mark our territories through planting of flags, installing borders, fences, signs, etc. And, just like animals, we engage in the defense and protection of those claims through posturing, intimidation, use of force, and aggression. Animals mark their territories so that other intruders of their particular species will know that a certain territory belongs to a certain animal or group of animals. We do the same.

As humans, we engage in territorial behavior constantly – at a micro level as well as at a macro level. We exhibit this instinctive behavior at a very young age. Approximately around the age of two, we start to recognize that we can lay claim to things around us and so we do (the "mine" stage), especially when it comes to toys and other play things. Anybody who has been around kids of this age has witnessed the drama and conflict that arises when one little kid wants to play with another kid's toys. The other kid may have many toys at his disposal, but he cannot let go of even one of his toys. Fighting over the toy, screaming, yelling, and crying are not uncommon responses in these situations. We are hard-wired to be territorial. Having spent time with my two nephews when they were around that age, I witnessed first-hand the epic battles of wills that ensued when they would suddenly find themselves in this territorial conundrum over some nondescript toy or object.

This instinctive territorial behavior follows us into our adult lives as we lay claim to various things including our property, our belongings, our cars, our dwellings, our families, our groups, our teams, our tribes. Unlike animals, however, who mark their territory via urine or glandular secretions, we instead mark our territory by building fences, walls, gates, moats, posting signs, flags, tagging, etc. to keep intruders at bay and to make others aware of the purview of our claims. We exhibit this territorial behavior at a micro level as individuals, but we also exhibit this at a macro level as nations. We, as a collective group of people, lay claim to land via colonization, annexation, and war. We then build borders to demarcate the claimed territory as belonging to us (as a collective group of people) and to keep intruders at bay. Then, we fly flags to indicate the laying of a claim having been established so that others may recognize the territory as belonging to a specific nation, which is another tribal marker. Additionally, we engage in a vast array of additional markers by adopting and employing certain symbols and symbolism to represent our territory and to signal to others the ownership thereof via official seals, emblems, colors, mottos, coats of arms, etc. These actions are the "modern" manifestations of innately imbedded behaviors. We, not unlike other animals in nature, have an innate need to practice territorialism. Unlike animals, however, we have very elaborate ways of marking these territorial claims and employ innumerable trappings and accoutrements that are corollaries of this behavior.

As a conjunctive product of this territorial behavior, we also display an innate need to exercise control and defend our claims once these have been marked and established. Just as animals display this behavior, we do so as well, albeit at a more sophisticated level of course (but not always). We do this via various means including shows of force, posturing, intimidation, and by engaging in actual conflict if necessary. Animals use their claws, teeth, and their horns or antlers to defend their claim. We use posturing via shows of strength through our military might and weapons arsenals, intimidation via military maneuvers and exercises, and ultimately through engaging in actual battle and war when necessary. These are behaviors that, like other instinctive behaviors, are also deeply imbedded in our DNA. Because of this, they exist within us as any other instinctive behavior does – often outside of the purview of our consciousness or awareness.

This instinct for territorialism and the commensurate defending behavior of that territory is at the root of much of our behaviors that are construed as racist and xenophobic. While racism certainly exists as previously stated, often the behaviors that we display towards others do not originate from purely racist tendencies or motivations. Many times the behaviors that are construed as racist, xenophobic, and bigoted stem from these underlying, innate, instinctive tendencies within us to protect and defend "our own," to protect and defend our territorial claims against rival tribes – those who are different in some shape or form from us, from the tribe to whom we belong. This is the essence of tribalism and tribalistic behavior.

Territorialism is an instinct. We act upon this instinct as other animals do. When we lay claim to a specific territory, we will engage in the commensurate accompanying behaviors by marking, defending, and, if necessary, use force to keep "intruders" at bay. The "intruders" is one of the elements that is at the crux of the matter for "who exactly are the intruders?" That, of course, depends on which tribe we belong to and espouse. It is where we find ourselves reverting to our primal tribal tendencies and, consequently, results in what can be regarded as discriminatory and racist behavior towards others – those "others" whom we regard as different than us and who are not part of our "tribe."

From the vantage point of the "home team" (those who claim original ownership status), the intruders can be anyone who falls outside the paradigm of an idealistic vision of what a "real American" is, which, for a significant part of American history, consisted of WASP (White, Anglo-Saxon, Protestant). This is a legacy that is still existent today, in a modified form, of course. It is a legacy that Donald Trump so deftly tapped into as he ascended into power and gained popularity amongst the masses who share in his views and beliefs regarding America.

PART THREE:

OUR TRIBES

OUR TRIBAL STANDING

From the vantage point of our modern day society, it is difficult for us to imagine or appreciate just how precarious and challenging life was for our ancestors in early human history. In our modern world, we have so many amenities, conveniences, and systems in place that mitigate the obstacles and rigors of daily living that it makes it very elusive to fully grasp what our earliest ancestors had to contend with in their normal everyday lives (we have a hard enough time imagining what our lives were like prior to cell phones!). Two hundred thousand years ago, if one was hungry, one could not just simply go to the corner convenience store on a whim to purchase a hot dog and a bag of chips to appease that hunger because there were no stores back then (much less hot dogs or chips – although some of our modern-day hot dogs may be able to survive that long!). One could not order a pizza to be delivered or have a food delivery service bring food from a store. What food one could acquire had to either be hunted or foraged and picked from the surrounding area. Finding food was an overarching and never-ending endeavor as the survival of the group depended on it and much of an individual's daily activities revolved around this imperative. The lives of our early ancestors were also very nomadic as they were constantly on the move in synchronicity with the migratory patterns of the herds they hunted and depended on for survival. (I don't suspect that many of us in our modern-day society base our relocation on the movement of our favorite food establishments, but I could be wrong – there are some people who are very passionate about their gastronomical preferences!). As daily life back then entailed the constant search for food in order to survive, it was apparent from very early that these functions were much more effective and successful when done collectively in groups. In such an environment where life was fraught with danger and harsh conditions, the chances of survival were much greater by banding together and working collaboratively with the members of our tribe as opposed to going alone and, thus, belonging to a group was essential for survival, it was essentially a survival mechanism.

Out of necessity, our early ancestors needed to band together into groups for survival and belonging to a group was of immense importance. Today, our survival is not necessarily contingent on belonging to any one particular group, however, we still carry this primal and compulsory need to belong and to be part of a group nevertheless. Even if it is no longer necessary for our survival, it is still eminently important for our social well-being. We have an innate compulsion to belong and we continually seek those groups which we can espouse as our own. When we find a group whose actions and ideologies align with our own, and when we actually join that group, we embrace the culture of the group and all of the trappings that go along with it wholeheartedly. In essence, we assimilate into the group.

In ancient times, banding into groups for the purposes of food-gathering and hunting was eminently important. It was also necessary for self-protection and defense against predators and other clans. Firearms were a distant reality in early human history so that a lone individual fending for himself or herself out in the wilderness would not fare very well for long armed with a club or a flint blade. He or she would not stand a chance of survival against a pack of hungry wolves, an attacking big cat or bear, or, for that matter, a pack of marauding humans. This vulnerability would have been exacerbated even more so in the darkness of nightfall prior to there being any means of artificial lighting. Before the invention of electricity or gas lamps or candles for that matter, nighttime darkness was a perilous condition as nocturnal predators skulked and prowled for opportunities to find prey. A lone individual fending for himself in the dark of night would find it a very tenuous enterprise. This danger would have been exacerbated even more so prior to our human ancestors developing the capacity to harness and control fire to, at the very least, have a campfire to provide some semblance of light. Darkness begot danger and a singular individual would have been susceptible to any number of hazards in such conditions. Beyond these inherent hazards presented by the environment, even illness would have been difficult to overcome without the care and assistance of others. Belonging to a group meant that one could be cared for and tended to by the other members of the group while recovering from illness or injury.

Amidst these precarious conditions, belonging to and being in a group greatly increased one's chances for survival. As such, staying in good standing with the group was eminently important and necessary in order to continue to be allowed to remain in the group and thereby ensure one's survival. In these hazardous times, being in good standing with the greater group was an incredibly important aspect of group dynamics. This entailed meeting numerous expectations and norms particular to the group including contributing to meet the basic needs of the group through cooperative work, cooperative hunts, and cooperative gathering of food. It also entailed cooperative protection of the group against potential threats. Being in and staying in good standing with one's tribe meant going to battle for the sake of the group – against predators and against other rival groups. We carry this innate drive to protect and defend our groups (verbally and physically) to this day. We defend our "tribes" against threats from other "tribes" – both real and perceived, including those threats that are contrived. We defend our "turf," that which we deem belongs to our tribe. The turf can be a literal physical area or territory that we claim as belonging to our tribe with specific boundaries as in prehistoric times where such a claim would have been a hunting ground. In more modern times, a turf could be a neighborhood, a community, or a country – all of which have specific borders and boundaries. The turf can also be an ideological turf such as a political ideology that we defend against attacks from "rival" tribes who are intent on attacking and undermining our belief systems and ideologies and, thereby, represent an existential threat to the tribe in that respect. These rival tribes are those whom we have a tendency to view as "intruders," those that are "not like us," those that are different than us – different from our tribe in some way, shape, or form. This lies at the locus of racist and discriminatory behavior.

DEFENDING OUR "TURF"

When we "defend our turf," we are, in essence, defending our tribe. As previously mentioned, our tribes come in many forms, shapes, and sizes, and, consequently, so do the "turfs" that belong to our tribes. A turf can be an actual parcel of land such as a neighborhood that is claimed by a gang for example, or it could be a more expansive territory such as those claimed by cartels, biker gangs, etc. A turf can be an ideological turf where the territory claimed is not necessarily of a physical nature, but rather, an allegorical space in people's hearts and minds in the form of beliefs and ideas such as political ideologies. In defending one's turf, one is protecting it against intruders – those who pose a threat to the tribe and what the tribe stands for. This is a behavior that we can all relate to as protecting our most basic tribe, our families, is universal. At a more macro level, a tribe's turf can be a neighborhood, a community, a region, or even an entire country for that matter. The tribes in this context and their respective turfs can be multifold. A tribe could be an actual gang that is defending the turf it claims for its own such as a particular neighborhood. The tribe could also be our family, our school our sports teams, our town, our city, our country – all of which are representative of a tribe in one form or another. A tribe's turf can also be ideological in nature and can encompass things such as political and religious beliefs.

A more modern iteration of the concept of defending one's turf is "protecting one's house." In this colloquialism, the "house" refers not only to a family's home, but also to the various other "homes" that we claim for our tribes – the allegorical homes. "This is our house!" is a commonly used refrain in our current popular culture that is proclaimed in this spirit of protecting and defending one's turf – the turf that belongs to our tribes. It is an expression used often in the context of sports where the home court, home field, home stadium, etc. belonging to a particular team is considered to be a place where the opposing team has no business entering much less with the expectation of coming out victorious. It is the attitude of protecting one's home court, an attitude that stems from primal tendencies where one, as a member of a tribe, would do everything possible to defend the tribe against another tribe – an invading tribe – even if it meant placing oneself in harm's way and, in the process, possibly make the ultimate sacrifice of giving one's life for the sake of the tribe.

A relatively recent marketing campaign conducted by the sportswear company, UnderArmour, took this notion of protecting one's turf and made it the central message of its advertisements. The message of "we must protect this house" was the theme of this marketing campaign. It revolved around members of a team having their pre-game "pep talk" and making it clear that no other team would be coming into their home court and come out victorious – not without a fight. A fight of epic proportions as if one was protecting one's own home against intruders, the intruders in this case being the opposing team and the "house" being the home team's court or field. This is another example of how savvy marketing and advertising firms are in tapping into our primal drivers as they recognize that this kind of messaging resonates with everyone. Who does not want to protect their house? We all do, of course. Brilliant!

Of course, this notion of protecting one's house applies not only to sports teams or a sports context exclusively, we apply this premise to other "houses" in our lives – other areas to which we lay claim and are meaningful for us. We see this play out quite vividly in a socio-political context in the way that people claim this country (or any country for that matter) as their own – their own turf, their land, their "house." In so doing, through the act of laying claim to the land (the turf), they are, in essence, planting their flag (literally and figuratively) to make it known that it belongs to them just as tribes have claimed a particular area for their own for thousands of years. It is a laying of claim of the land, but also a commensurate laying of claim to the ideologies, customs, and practices of the tribe to whom the land belongs. In the case of these United States, the literal turf is the actual physical expanse of land that constitutes the country itself and the commensurate figurative turf consists of the ideals which are regarded as encapsulating the "American" way of life, those which were established at the founding of the nation and which have been upheld, executed, and handed down over time. If anybody or any group does not abide by, embrace, or otherwise exemplify these ideals, then that person can be construed as not being truly "American."

Consequently, that individual or group represents a threat to the American way of life and must be treated accordingly – with disdain, disgust, and distrust – as would be the automatic response of any tribe intent on maintaining group cohesion. Such is a response that is ingrained within us and forged over millennia in order to keep the integrity of the group dynamic. To do otherwise threatens the integrity and cohesion of the group and its ability to function properly as a collective group of people. We carry this internal impulsive behavior and is exhibited consistently in numerous contexts.

This notion of maintaining and reinforcing group cohesion is exemplified in various ways in our everyday lives at a micro-level and also at a macro-level through the policies and practices that are implemented to conserve and uphold this concept and executed to foster unity and reinforce the integrity of the collective, the tribe – in this case, the tribe being the nation itself. Group cohesion is fostered and maintained through commonly adopted practices such as recitation of the pledge of allegiance, singing of the national anthem at public gatherings, observation of specific holidays and commemorative dates, specific public ceremonies, as well as the use and display of the American flag in numerous forms.

This notion of protecting one's house is something that we carry within us and have employed for thousands of years so it should not surprise us when it is executed and whenever it is invoked by any one group or tribe. In essence, it is an essential component of a well-functioning and cohesive collective (tribe) and applicable regardless of size (it's just as necessary for a family unit as it is for a nation-state). It is, however, a much more complex issue in the context of a nation as there are many additional factors to take into consideration in this respect.

CLAIMING ONE'S HOOD

Growing up in Tucson, Arizona, I came to understand the significance that various neighborhoods held for some people and the affiliation that was ascribed to these neighborhoods as their community of origin or their adopted community. Various people would talk about being from or growing up in a specific community or a specific barrio. Whether it was Barrio Anita, Barrio Hollywood, Barrio Viejo, South Park, OP (Old Pascua), New Pascua, etc., people would talk with pride and nostalgia about being from one of these particular communities located throughout town. I never quite came to fully know the specific boundaries that encompassed all of these neighborhoods, but I understood that these communities held a particular significance and meaning for those who "claimed" them – for those who lived or grew up in these neighborhoods. There was a discernable and palpable sense of loyalty and devotion that people held for these communities as they talked about them. These communities were, in essence, "their people." In a sense, they represented their tribes.

I believe that for many of us, we hold an affinity and a sense of nostalgia for the places in which we were raised – even if those places were not the greatest places in which to grow up whether due to crime, drugs, gang activity, etc. However, all of those inherent characteristics of a community, whether good or bad, allow for a collective experience for those who live in the community and it is in that collective experience that we develop a sense of group identity, a sentiment that "we are all in this together." We share in the struggle together as well as the joys. These experiences help to shape us as individuals and also as a community. The community rises and falls with the various experiences that it undergoes and foments collective bonds of shared experience amongst its members. We celebrate and mourn together when something occurs that impacts the community as a whole. It is no wonder why we develop such strong ties to our neighborhoods, our communities in which we were raised – even if they were rough communities in which to grow up and even if the times were tough when we lived there. It seems that this is a generally ubiquitous sentiment amongst people and it is especially true if one is ever displaced from his or her community of origin at some point in time in one's life.

I came to understand that this act of "claiming" a particular neighborhood was a way to indicate which "tribe" one belonged to. It was also a way to legitimize one's longstanding roots in a certain region (being a local v. a newbie) as well as to legitimize one's genuineness and notion of being perceived as "real" and unpretentious.

Living in or having grown up in a particular neighborhood or barrio was a way to legitimize one's "street cred;" a way to show to others that one was not coddled or spoiled growing up; that he or she was streetwise and knew how to relate to others without pretense or facades. All of which made one real…..and tough, and not prone to being easily intimidated nor to suffer fools lightly.

It is a commonly accepted notion that, in order to have "street cred," you have to have a community from which you hail that legitimizes that street cred. As such, you have to "claim a hood" – a neighborhood in which one grows up that is real and unpretentious containing its share of inherent challenges and struggles. By the same token, it would be very difficult for a person to claim to have street cred if he or she grew up in an affluent neighborhood devoid of the struggles and tribulations that builds a tough skin and resilient spirit – nobody has ever claimed Beverly Hills or Bel Air as their "hood" in order to legitimize their street cred. Namely because those communities represent the opposite of a place where one can develop street cred; they represent the opposite of a "hood."

In a sense, claiming a hood is essentially claiming one's tribe and the larger group to whom we feel a sense of belonging and fealty. This is a notion that we engage in consistently as a people and constantly throughout our lifetimes. We are continuously "claiming a hood." That hood could be our families, our neighborhood, the towns and cities in which we live, our state, our teams, the clubs and organizations that we belong to, our faith communities, our political parties, or our nation. The hoods that we claim can be multiple and ever expansive.

We are intrinsically social creatures and, as social creatures, we are hard-wired with a primal need to belong to a group – to "claim our hoods," as it were. As such, the social circles to which we belong are of immense importance to us – even to the point of use of force and violence to defend and protect them, which happens consistently in the context of defending and protecting our communities – our turfs – as well as in the context of defending and protecting our ideological hoods. Sadly, this is too often carried out through acts of violence against others – those whom one tribe views as representing an existential threat by the mere act of belonging to the "other" side – the other tribe.

GROUP NORMS

Throughout the span of our lives, we become a part of numerous different groups, both by choice and, at times, by de facto. We are born into a group, our family, and, as we grow, we join other groups including educational institutions, school clubs, sports teams, our jobs, neighborhood associations, civic groups, fraternal orders, political groups, parenting groups, trade groups, unions, etc. There exist a vast number of groups that one can be a part of across the span of one's lifetime.

We join a group from the very onset. From the very beginning of our lives, we are born into a group, that being our families. This is a group that, for most of us, will remain the most important group throughout our lives. Being our most important group, we go to extreme lengths to protect it, care for it, and defend it. The vast majority of us would give our lives to defend and protect our families if it were necessary. As our most important group, most of us strive to be in good standing with this our primary group by being supportive, caring, and responsive in times of need to the members of our family.

In ancient times, being ostracized from one's most important and critical group would have been a life-threatening scenario as all the safety and security rendered from belonging to the group would have been dissolved. In our modern-day society, we still carry an intrinsic aversion to being ostracized from the important groups to which we belong and will do everything we can to avoid that if possible. It stems from a desire to belong and be accepted that we carry to this day. And, in order to be accepted, it entails adopting the norms of the group.

Whether by choice or through osmosis, many of us adopt and share the same set of beliefs and values held by the most important and primary group in our lives, our families. This makes sense as, for most of us, this is the group with which we spend most of our time, to which we have most exposure, and is typically the group with the most influence on us, especially during our formative years. As such, we acquire and adopt many of the intrinsic traits of this, our primary group, including norms, attitudes, and beliefs around faith, community, nation, politics, etc. We even adopt the mannerisms, expressions (both verbal and non-verbal), and dialect of our familial groups. And thus, the beliefs of the family group generally become our own beliefs as well. The views of the family become our views. The proclivities of the family become our own proclivities. The attitudes of the family group become our own attitudes. In this way, the familial unit is able to function in an effective and cohesive manner. Without this as a foundational premise of the group, it is much more challenging for any group to function as a unit including our families. It becomes much more difficult to function effectively if there exists discord and dissonance amongst the unit – if there exists disunity amongst the group members, especially when it concerns core values and beliefs. And so, for the most part, familial units are, by necessity, typically very homogenous in regards to its intrinsic attributes, its values, and its beliefs.

For most of us, familial beliefs and values are passed on and adopted through a combination of osmosis, influence, instruction, and even indoctrination. As members of a particular family, we come to value the same values and beliefs that are important to the family – including those pertaining to faith, nation, education, work, and politics. In this way, a common corollary emerges where, if our family is politically aligned with the Democratic party, we grow up with Democratic party values and have a greater propensity to align and identify ourselves as Democrats. The same holds true if the family in which we were raised affiliates itself with the Republican party. We then grow up with Republican values and align ourselves as such. Likewise, if our family is Catholic, we then are more likely to be Catholic. If our family is Protestant, Jewish, Buddhist, etc., then we are more likely to affiliate ourselves with those respective faiths. This even applies to choice of profession, choice of schools, military service, choice of teams to root for, etc. I have always found it inter-esting that, in certain families, there exists a longstanding tradition of choosing to work in certain professions that spans generations such as law enforcement, fire-fighting, health care, teaching, etc. Living and growing up in such families, one comes to recognize that this is something that the family unit considers worthy and noble as evidenced by the longstanding tradition amidst the family lineage.

Children growing up in such an environment come to recognize these professions as having high value within the family circle and, thus, likewise choose to follow in those footsteps. I have witnessed this principle applied in a variety of ways whereby the children growing up in a particular family will reflect the family's loyalties in various forms.

In my family, my sister-in-law grew up in a home where her father was (and continues to be) a staunch Oakland Raiders (now known as the Las Vegas Raiders) and University of Arizona Wildcats fan. Growing up in this environment where her dad placed a high value on these team affiliations, she also became a fan for the same teams so that, as an adult, she is also a Raiders fan as well as Wildcats fan. Such is the case for other groups with which a family unit identifies. If we grow up in a family that roots and supports Notre Dame football, the Boston Red Sox, or Iowa Hawkeye Wrestling, for example, we are more likely to align our loyalties to those team affiliations as well.

We also see this familial influence phenomenon apply to not so noble pursuits such gang affiliation where, if a family identifies with a certain gang identity, then a person growing up in such an environment will identify with a particular gang identity as well. It becomes part of the ethos of the family and an expectation that is unfairly placed on those growing up in such a family culture. Over the years, I have seen my share of families where every member of the family wore red, an indication of their affiliation to or desire to be affiliated with the Bloods. I'm sure that it is also the case with wearing blue as an indication of an affiliation with the Crips, however, growing up in Tucson, that was not as common to see.

It's hard to go against the grain of our most important group, our families, lest we cause a lot of friction and discord. If ever these core values are rejected by a member of the group, it can have the effect of upsetting the cohesiveness of the group and the collaboration amongst its members which is necessary for it to function effectively. It can even lead to being shunned and ostracized from the group in the interest of the greater whole. This dynamic translates to other groups to which we belong as well including our work groups, civic groups, political groups, faith communities, etc. For some individuals, unfortunately, their family group is non-existent or severely dysfunctional and might as well be non-existent. For persons who find themselves in these situations, they often seek out a surrogate group to replace this important base group. The surrogate group then becomes their adopted "family" and oftentimes is referred to as such. The surrogate family can be a gang, a support group, a social group, etc.

You may be reading this and thinking: "I don't agree with this premise because I went against everything that my family believed and stood for!" And, yes, that happens too. Some of us consciously rebel against the norms and values of the families in which we grew up, for a variety of reasons. Some of us represent the Alex P. Keaton of our families (as you may remember from that particular sitcom, "Family Ties," Alex, the son, played by Michael J. Fox, was the antithesis of what his parents held dear, they being former hippies and left-leaning liberals whereas he was the epitome of a capitalistic, socially conservative Republican). And, yes, these dynamics also happen, but, for the most part, we take on the identity of the family in which we were raised and adopt the same or similar set of familial values and beliefs as adults.

One of the major benefits of going to college or military service (and especially through living in another country for a period of time as is the case with study abroad programs and foreign service such as Peace Corps) is that it provides an individual with the opportunity to gain exposure and interact with persons different than oneself outside of the family unit – to persons of different backgrounds, ethnicities, religious beliefs, different cultures, different upbringing – who have different perspectives and life experiences. In this way, one can expand his/her horizons in this manner and learn about other ways of thinking including new ideas and new experiences. Without this opportunity for exposure to people who are different than ourselves and different than what we have known thus far, it is a very difficult leap for us to appreciate and be empathetic to those who are different from us. It is very difficult to supersede our innate proclivities for tribalism and the commensurate tribal behaviors that accompany them. This limit of exposure most often occurs naturally by the intrinsic composition of the communities in which we are raised, however, it also happens by design as communities are, at times, developed with this isolationist and exclusionary purpose in mind as has happened in the past via the practice of redlining whereby certain neighborhoods, through systemic discriminatory practices, had the effect of de facto segregation by denying access to credit and mortgages to people of color, thereby resulting in predominantly white communities – an institutionally-implemented level of control as to who was allowed to live in certain communities and who was not. This also happens in our modern day environment via less insidious yet still exclusionary practices such as the development of isolationist and "planned" communities located in specific areas across the country as well as, to some extent, through age-restricted communities and gated communities.

PART FOUR:

RACISM & LAW- ENFORCEMENT

THE THIN BLUE LINE

Our innate instincts and proclivities influence a lot of our behaviors, often in ways of which we are not fully aware or cognizant thereof. Taking these compulsions and propensities that we carry within us into account, it makes conducting some professions much more difficult and challenging than others. For those who work in law enforcement, they are charged with a nearly impossible task of compulsory modulation of their innate instincts – for tribalism, collectivism, differentiation, etc. They are also expected to modulate their inner fight or flight response at a level that is quite unreasonable as they engage with individuals who are also functioning within the realm of their primal limbic system and are also in a state of fight or flight.

Viewing the profession from this perspective, it is no wonder that encounters between law-enforcement and civilians go awry as often as they do.

Most of us have a job where we go to work with the innate understanding that, unless something extremely out of the ordinary were to take place, our lives are not in danger. As we engage with clients, customers, patients, students, co-workers, staff, etc., we are not called to function primarily from a state of fight or flight. Unless one is an emergency responder or deployed military member, our work routines are such that most of us can go about our day without much eventfulness. We pretty much know what to expect from day to day as we execute our given tasks, duties, and responsibilities. Now imagine going to work knowing full well that you may encounter a situation or several situations in the course of your work day where your life may be put in danger. And imagine that this is a norm in your daily work life. Such is the case for our law enforcement personnel.

Law enforcement officers are first and foremost human beings just like the rest of us. As such, they have the same primal tendencies that we all have. Just as the rest of us, they are also functioning in a modern world with anciently developed instincts and proclivities. The challenge for them and others in similar professions is that they are functioning in a constant state of fight or flight as a matter of course for their profession. For most of us, we are not called upon to function primarily from a place of the primal, limbic system of the brain, on a daily basis as they do. Day in and day out, they have to engage their primal and instinctive response of fight or flight as they carry out their jobs. However, flight is not an option. Instead, they have to suppress the flight part of that binary instinctual phenomenon and resort to a fight response exclusively. Their training is predicated on this. They are not trained to flee a scene of danger. Quite the opposite, they are trained to approach and infiltrate scenes of danger so that the danger can be quelled and mitigated. This involves the fight response. This involves the fight response using weapons. This involves the fight response using weapons, the primary weapon being a firearm. That mistakes happen in encounters with law enforcement is undeniable. As imperfect beings, we are all prone to making mistakes. However, given the nature of the extreme set of circumstances that take place in encounters with law enforcement, the stakes are very high. When mistakes happen in such circumstances, the resulting outcomes can be deadly. And tragic.

As a society, we have certain expectations and standards that we hold for certain professions. We expect our faith leaders to be moral, we expect judges to be fair and impartial, we expect our educators to be knowledgeable, we expect physicians to be competent, we expect counselors to be empathetic, we expect our military personnel to be courageous. When it comes to our law enforcement personnel, we expect all of these qualities and more. In addition to these qualities, we expect them to be responsive and available at a moment's notice when we need them. We expect them to arrive quickly when called upon. We expect them to conduct themselves with professionalism. We expect them to take control of difficult situations. We expect them to mitigate and/or eliminate dangers and dangerous situations. We expect them to protect us. Additionally, when not responding to emergencies, we expect them to be friendly, courteous, and approachable. We expect them to engage with the community. We expect a lot from them, somewhat unreasonably so.

GOOD COP, BAD COP

Something happens to people in positions of authority. Most of us at some point in our lives have experienced an encounter with a person in a position of authority that left us feeling less than optimal. The reality is that some people take the authority bestowed upon them and push it to the limits of what would be considered appropriate and proper. Some people abuse it outright. At times for their own personal gain. At times to oppress, repress, and be abusive to others. It's a phenomenon that occurs to some individuals when they hold a position of societally accepted clout, status, and power over others. At times, this is situational, at times it is systemic. This can happen in any profession. We learn all too frequently from the news media how certain individuals have taken their position of power and authority to abuse other people. The #MeToo movement shed quite a bright light on the abuse that many women have had to endure at the hands of men where a power differential existed. Such was the case involving Olympic gymnasts and the gymnastics team doctor, Larry Nasser. Such was the case with Jeffrey Epstein, Harvey Weinstein, and in so many other situations – both public and private in nature.

Law enforcement is not exempt from this sociological phenomenon of abuse of power and authority. Although, as previously mentioned, when it pertains to law enforcement, the stakes are much higher than most other professions because of the nature of the job, the tools of the trade, and the use of force often involved to carry out the job. Additionally, when it pertains to law enforcement, the power differential between officer and civilian is much greater than most situations in which a power differential exists, especially because lethal weapons are involved. In just about any encounter with law enforcement, the officers are the ones in control – they hold the power. This is understood. That is how they are trained. To not be in control can create a life-threatening situation for them so they must exercise a high level of control at all times – control over persons and of situations. Often, for those on the receiving end, this can be perceived as intimidation and unnecessary aggression.

The challenge is that the law enforcement profession carries with it much weight, clout, and power. Additionally, law enforcement personnel also have lethal weapons at their disposal which they can brandish when necessary to compel a person to follow their commands, by force if necessary. They also carry the ability to apprehend and make an arrest when such is called for. These factors create a significant automatic power differential whenever there is an encounter with a law enforcement officer and a civilian.

For the vast majority of us, we engage in behavior that is very deferential when it involves encounters with law enforcement personnel because of this inherent power differential. It is a widely understood societal norm that we follow. To do otherwise would risk increasing the likelihood of being cited and/or arrested, and, for many people of color, the resulting outcomes could be much worse than that. Too often, we learn about these encounters going awry through the media and the resulting tragic outcomes thereof. So much so that, for many people, they view all law enforcement personnel through a lens of distrust and suspicion. It is a sad commentary of the times in which we live. However, if we take into consideration the elements described which are present in these encounters, it provides us with a wider scope of understanding. It may not ultimately change our views, but at least we can consider the numerous factors involved in these matters. Often, there are numerous factors involved other than racism or racist motivations in these encounters. Sometimes, what we construe as racism stems from innate primal tendencies that appear racially motivated when, in reality, they are primally motivated – executed as a result of innate instincts and nothing more. Of course, this is no consolation when things go awry.

PRIMAL OVERRIDE

I don't pretend to know what it's like to be a police officer as I have never been one. However, I know what it's like to be human with human tendencies and inclinations....and primal behaviors.

Throughout my professional working career, I have worked primarily in the field of human services and primarily via non-profit organizations. In the course of carrying out this work, I have, at different times, worked in certain settings that were considered to have a large proportion of at risk youth. The "at risk" label carries with it a lot of negative connotations that does not accurately or fairly describe the kind of kids I encountered, however, as I found the vast majority of them to have been very sweet, fun, and interesting kids.

Even so, having worked with challenging and high risk communities and populations, in all my professional career, in the various jobs that I've held, I cannot recall even one moment where I felt that my life was in danger. And yet, for law enforcement personnel, the risk of putting one's life and limb in danger as part of their job is a veritable reality. Every time they put on their uniform and every time they don their badge, they are cognizant that they could very well face a life-threatening situation in the course of carrying out their work on any given day. Because of this potentiality, they have to conduct themselves at a heightened level of alertness every time they answer a call or make a stop. Their life may very well depend on it. I could not imagine having a profession where one has to function at this heightened mental state at all times knowing full well that to do otherwise, to let one's guard down even one time could result in tragedy. Such is the reality for law enforcement personnel.

I consider myself to be pretty cool and collected. I have a very easy going nature and don't anger easily. However, even though I have those intrinsic qualities as part of my personality, I am not exempt from losing my composure on occasion. It happens. It happens to the best of us. However, even when I have lost my composure, I don't lose control of my faculties.....except once. I can recall a situation that highlighted this for me and has stayed with me because of it. It so happened several years ago when my sister was pregnant with my nephew who is now a teenager. It was a Sunday afternoon and she, my mom, and I went to eat lunch at a local Mexican restaurant. It had been a family tradition for us to go out to eat on Sundays for many years. As we were reviewing the menu and eating our chips and salsa prior to ordering, a young guy and what seemed to be his mother were sitting at another table close to us. At some point in the course of our family conversation, something must have been said where the young guy felt the need to interject in a way that my sister did not see quite fit. So, being of a strong nature, she retorted to him. He then, retorted back at her. As the situation turned argumentative, name-calling ensued and it was at that point where I lost it. I remember getting up as I started yelling at the guy and challenging him to go outside to fight. Of course this caused the scene to get totally out of control where now both factions were yelling and trying to quell the situation. As the guy and his mother walked out, I remember her snidely remarking to me that I had anger management issues (which is as far from the truth as can be). Of course, at that point, we left the restaurant as well. Nobody was in the mood to have a family meal anymore.

This situation stayed with me for several reasons but mainly because I experienced something very strange and foreign to me. I can still recall the scene, but even as I re-live it in my mind, I can remember the strange sensation of not being in control of my faculties, my actions, or my words as if I were watching a character in a movie. I was reacting and saying things that I don't normally do or say; in a way that was very out of character for me. It was like having an out of body experience and being aware of it even while it was happening, yet not being able to control it, as if somebody else was controlling me and my actions. As if somebody had a remote control and was pushing certain buttons to direct my words and deeds and making me do certain things in spite of myself. It was quite a strange sensation. Of course, looking back with the benefit of hindsight and a better understanding and knowledge of our inherent primal tendencies, I now recognize it for what it was. It was a perfect example of the primal portion of my brain taking over. The limbic portion of my brain took charge of the situation, pushing the reasoning and inhibitive, "higher functioning" portion of my brain aside in response to a fight or flight situation. And it wanted me to fight.

Reflecting on that situation and thinking about how quickly it escalated and got out of hand, I can imagine what it would have been like if either he or I had a gun at the time. One, or both of us, would have probably pulled out our weapon if for nothing more than to intimidate each other and make the other person back down. Having experienced that out of body sensation first-hand where I was not in control of myself, I can also imagine how often situations such as this take place in our society. How often do people find themselves in highly charged situations where the primal, limbic system of their brain takes over and they lose control of their normal behavioral tendencies – of their capacity to exercise reasoning, restraint, and inhibitive behavior. We are all prone to this as there is a limbic system that resides within all of us. We are all prone to its capacity to take over in highly charged, volatile situations. That is what it was designed to do as, in a situation of immediate and present danger, taking the time to think and contemplate about the best course of action would have led to certain death or harm. Sometimes, there just isn't any time to think, there is only time to only react. That is what it's there for. We are all prone to lose control of ourselves as the primal portion of our brain overrides our higher functioning cerebral cortex and we engage in actions that we would not normally do under more normal circumstances.

I think about this, of my personal experience of losing control of my faculties at the hand of the primal portion of my brain, and contemplate what it must be like for law enforcement personnel to have to engage in such highly charged situations on a regular basis. How often do they have to deal with individuals who are not in control of their faculties? How often do they have to deal with individuals operating from the primal, limbic system of their brain? How often do they themselves, not just as law enforcement personnel but simply as human beings, also experience the override of their central nervous system by the limbic system in highly charged scenarios in the course of their work? The nature of their work calls upon them to intentionally put themselves in such volatile situations and it would seem nearly impossible to maintain one's composure day in and day out over the course of years as they carry out their jobs. That is not our natural tendency. And yet, such is asked of them. And to do so over the course of their careers which could last for decades.

We are all prone to the vicissitudes of the primal brain within all of us. Law enforcement personnel are no exception. However, not all of us are placed in such highly charged, dangerous, unpredictable situations on a consistent basis as they are. Also, not all of us are called upon to have to use force and/or firearms as part of our jobs like they are called to do. Highly charged, volatile situations are unpredictable due to the very challenging nature of the situations and the variance of emotional and mental states of the individuals involved. When people are not in their right frame of mind, when they are not in control of their faculties, when the limbic system overrides their central nervous system, people can act and react in unpredictable and erratic ways. In ways that are out of character for the person as was the case with me. It is extremely difficult to deal with people and to reason with them when they are in such a state. I certainly was in no condition to be reasoned with in my agitated state.

When a person is in a state of fight or flight, that is a recipe for disaster when dealing with law enforcement personnel. Law enforcement personnel are trained and equipped to deal with a person who is in a fight response with deadly force, especially if that person is being combative and threatening towards the officer or other persons at the scene and even more so if the person has a weapon. Law enforcement personnel are also trained to deal with a person in a flight response, those who flee from officers, with often similar force and deadly outcomes. That mistakes happen in these highly charged and volatile situations is not surprising. Many times these scenarios take place in an instant with no time to collect one's thoughts or contemplate the best or most prudent course of action. There is simply no time for that. Many of these situations unfold in an instant requiring instant reactions and responses. Of course, that is no consolation to those whose lives are affected when these encounters occur and go awry.

When a person does fall victim to a tragedy at the hands of law enforcement officers, it is tragic first and foremost. It is also understandable to place the blame on those officers involved. The blame may very well be warranted and justice may be necessary and called for according to each specific situation. As a person who recognizes how easy it is to lose control at the hands of my limbic, primal brain, I can recognize that these unfortunate situations are not always clear cut nor clearly defined; that there isn't always a simple reason or reasons for the outcome of these situations; that there are usually multiple factors at play – some very difficult and challenging ones where most of us would have a difficult time managing such volatile situations. These are not easy situations to manage by any means when one is embroiled in the midst of them and also not easy to manage by any means afterwards when they occur. The effect of these situations on people's lives is multifold.

Mistakes indeed do happen. Sometimes, there is an attempt to cover up mistakes when they occur, which only makes things worse. It is important to keep in mind, however difficult it may be, that these are extremely challenging jobs often dealing with extremely challenging situations with many factors at play. This doesn't dismiss the tragic nature of the outcomes. However, when viewing these from the perspective of primal reactions on behalf of both parties involved, the outcomes are not always clearly defined as to whom is responsible. Sometimes, it is our limbic system and our primal drivers that are ultimately responsible in these matters.

OUR PENCHANT
FOR CATEGORIZATION

n our Western society, we have quite an affinity for labeling and categorizing things and placing them neatly in the metaphorical boxes of our minds. We have a penchant for categorizing. Things that are nuanced, nebulous, amorphous, and difficult to categorize makes us mentally flustered as it challenges this paradigm. We want things to fit where we deem they should fit in our minds – where it makes sense in our heads they should fit. When things don't fit quite so neatly, it is disorienting for us and we have an aversion to feeling disoriented and confused. We engage in this penchant for categorization in many ways and apply it in a myriad of contexts: from music, to art, to film, food, literature, etc. We, especially in our Western society, like to categorize. When we cannot neatly and easily categorize things into genres, types, and classifications, it messes with our heads. We become discombobulated.

We apply this penchant for labeling and categorizing to people as well – groups of people as well as individuals. We categorize groups of people in many ways, whether by race, ethnicity, religion, gender, age......we have innumerable ways of categorizing one another. We categorize groups and we also categorize individuals. We categorize and label individuals by their persona, their attributes, their character, and their personality. We label people as easy-going, cheerful, high-maintenance, moody, nice, sweet, intelligent, mean. Just like the previously mentioned items, we categorize people so that it makes sense for us in our minds – so that we know how to deal and interact with that particular person. If we categorize a particular person as friendly, we know what interactions to expect from that person. Likewise, if we categorize a person as moody and difficult to deal with, then we know what to expect from our interactions with that person as well.

In addition to these informal categorizations, there is also institutional categorization. People are categorized according to race, ethnicity, gender, veteran status, age, income, education, political party, profession, etc. It has become such an accepted practice in our lives that we don't even think about it much as we fill out job applications, insurance documents, applications for assistive programs, surveys, questionnaires, product warranties, voter registrations, and other forms where we are asked to select from any number of categories with which we identify and deem fit such as: Hispanic, White, Black,

Asian, male, female, married, single, and so on. This is a practice that is engrained in our society.

Similarly, we also have the tendency to box and categorize people as either good or bad: "good guys v. bad guys," "cops v. robbers," "superheroes v. villains," "heels v. heroes," "good guy with a gun v. a bad guy with gun." We have a tendency for making binary judgements and labeling people as being either good or bad. The fact of the matter is that we, as humans, are much more complicated and much more nuanced than that. There are many factors that make us who we are as persons. However, that is difficult for many of us to contend with. As previously alluded, we have an innate tendency to place people in neat and tidy boxes as many of us have a much easier time viewing things in binary paradigms – it is simpler that way and we don't have to take all the various aspects of a person or thing into account. Nuanced shades are more difficult for us to navigate than simple black and white, good v. bad, hero v. villain. Moreover, we also have a tendency to ascribe labels to groups as an extension of our interactions with a representative of that group. When we have an interaction, whether positive or negative, with a person of a particular group, it creates in us a repository of good will or bad faith in the overall group that is represented by that person. The more of one type of interaction or another that we experience, the more that repository is reinforced with positive or negative impressions of that particular group. The way the media covers these portrayals also plays a large role in our developing positive or negative impressions of particular groups.

When it comes to law enforcement personnel, we apply the same principle and we make a distinction between "good cops" and "bad cops." This way, it is easier for us to process in our heads and make sense of actions that law enforcement take in the course of their work.

I believe that the vast majority of individuals who go into law enforcement do so with sincere motives and intentions as do the vast majority of educators, lawyers, nurses, social workers, engineers, architects and so on. People gravitate towards professions for which they feel an innate interest, a natural aptitude for, and a calling of some form or another. To go into a profession that one dislikes or has no interest or affinity for would be extremely counterintuitive and counterproductive. It would also foster a lot of misery for that person (and those around him/her). This may happen from time to time due to familial pressures and other extenuating circumstances, however, in our modern society, where individualism and personal agency is consistently extolled and highly regarded, the former would be the anomaly and the latter is the norm. There also exist numerous obstacles to conquer and steps to accomplish on the path towards most professions in the form of education and training prior to entering a particular profession. This also serves as a form of vetting for those who are truly invested in the profession they seek to enter. For these reasons, it makes it incredibly difficult for a person with nefarious intentions to enter a profession such as law enforcement with the premeditated and purposeful intent of doing harm to others. Does it never happen? Anything is possible, of course, but these would deem to be the rare exceptions. However, when situations go awry in encounters with law-enforcement personnel, it is our inclination to make a default judgement and label the officer involved as a "bad cop" when in reality it may have been a tragic outcome to a very challenging set of circumstances that took place.

Are there individuals who are unethical and conduct themselves inappropriately who work in law enforcement? Yes, of course.

Unfortunately, this takes place in any profession or walk of life. Often, however, our view of the whole is tainted by actions of a small minority and the tragic outcomes of those who commit such acts. Additionally, as previously mentioned, when such conduct takes place in the context of law enforcement, the tools of their trade make for much more lethal and tragic outcomes than most other professions. The vast majority of professions do not make the evening news when somebody's work project or assignment goes awry as it happens with law enforcement personnel. Also, the vast majority of professions do not have to carry weapons as part of their job nor do they involve having to put one's life at risk as part of the everyday duties and responsibilities of that job.

PART FIVE

RESILIENCE OF RACIST BEHAVIOR

MANUFACTURED
DIFFERENTIATION

In our American society, it is not very difficult to rcognize differences amongst people due to it being such a heterogeneous society. There is so much diversity in this country with so many individuals from places all over the world that differences abound. This is not the case in other countries and in other societies. The United States has been the great melting pot for generations and continues to be so as people from all over the world have come to this country seeking fortunes and opportunities for a better life (as well as safety as is the case with resettled populations fleeing war and violence in their home countries). Other countries, for the most part, have not offered such opportunities and, therefore, have not experienced the levels of immigration that the United States has since its inception. Because of this, other nations have much more homogenous populations and are less diverse. And yet, even in the absence of racial or ethnic diversity, people in these more homogenous societies still find ways to recognize differences amongst each other and engage in mistreatment, abuse, oppression, and exploitation of others because of those differences.

Being originally from Mexico, I have traveled there often throughout the years, primarily to visit family and relatives. Over the course of years traveling to and from Mexico, something that I always found interesting whenever I would visit was the stark contrast in the composition of its population compared to that of the United States. Whereas in the United States there are people from all corners of the world with a rich variety of ethnicities, cultures, languages, etc., in Mexico the population was much less diverse and much more homogenous overall (with the exception of certain pockets of the country that draw American expats and other nationalities, especially in beachside and retirement communities). This, of course, happens for many different reasons but, primarily, because the United States is a country with a rich history of immigration (forced and unforced) and has attracted and incentivized immigrants to support the founding and industrial development of the country over the years (much less so beginning in the latter part of the 20th century). I always found this diversity very appealing and something that I found myself taking for granted most of the time growing up in the United States. It was those times, upon returning from my travels to Mexico, that I would once again feel a deep sense of appreciation for the diversity that the United States has to offer in this respect. And yet, even though Mexico is a country that has a much higher level of homogeneity than the United States, people still find ways to differentiate themselves from one another and to focus on the presenting differences that exist amongst each other including differences in socioeconomic status, religious denomination, skin tone, and whether one hails from the city or the countryside (rural v. urban), amongst others.

I experienced this kind of tribalism first-hand. Having been born in a large, cosmopolitan city in the Southern part of Mexico close to Mexico City, I spent the first years of my life in a bustling, urban environment. Then, around the age of six, my family decided to move from our urban cityscape of origin to the Northern part of Mexico to the state of Sonora where work in the copper mines was abundant and where my dad worked for a period of time as a miner. As a little kid, I really didn't appreciate just how big this move was in so many respects. When you're a kid, everything is pretty much an adventure and you just go with the flow, especially as you really don't have much of a say in the matter. I think that if I had been older and, especially if I had been a teenager, the move would have been a much bigger deal for me (and my younger sister) and I would have most likely been very distraught at the prospect of leaving so much behind including my grandparents, aunts and uncles, cousins, friends, my neighborhood, and my school. Looking back now as an adult, it was quite a stark and momentous decision that my parents made as it was a total uprooting from everything we had known up until then.

Going from a large, metropolitan city in the heart of Mexico to a tiny rural town in the Northernmost part of the country was quite a drastic change. There were so many things that were different than what I had known in my hometown: the food was different, the way people dressed was different, the way people spoke and expressed themselves was different, the way of life was different. As for me, being a naïve little kid, I was oblivious to all of these differences at the time and just went about my days without much thought or concern and started attending the only school that existed in the town. It was not uncommon to encounter livestock on the way to school in this little town which had no traffic lights and no paved roads. Soon enough, however, some kids started calling me names because I was from a different part of the country, I was an outsider in their eyes. I realize now that I must have seemed as being quite different by the other kids. I wore my hair longer than they did (not by my choice, my parents had been forged by the culture of the sixties and had a more free-flowing attitude in that regard), wore a different style of clothes, different shoes, and I'm sure that I sounded differently than they did in the way I spoke. It was a recipe for being picked on. I wasn't targeted because of my race because we were all of the same race, nevertheless, the other differences that I represented were enough to draw derision and name-calling. It seems that we, as humans, always find a way to see the differences amongst each other even when we share the same race, ethnicity, culture, and language.

Sometimes, the differences that we represent occur naturally as was my case in moving from one region of the country to another, and, other times, we manufacture our differences. I think about the way that neighborhoods give rise to gangs and gang culture in so many cities across the country. Gang activity is a reality for many communities. Sadly, it is in this context that so much "black on black" violence occurs (as well as "brown on brown" violence).

When looking at the general demographic composition of communities and neighborhoods where rampant gang activity exists, the composition is generally homogenous overall. The demographics of a certain community could be predominantly black, or Latinx, or purple for that matter. Everybody could be primarily of one specific race or ethnicity and yet, that is not sufficient to foster camaraderie amongst all who reside there. In our hyper-racism-aware society, one would think that, because people share this general trait or commonality, that strife and discord would be minimal or non-existent. That people would be more apt to get along and live in harmony with one another. And yet, that is not the case. People still find a way to differentiate themselves from each other and to be at odds with each other in spite of being of the same race or ethnicity, speaking the same language, being of the same heritage, having the same socio-economic status, living in the same environment, facing the same set of challenges, etc. I think about the way that groups are forged in this context and how they go about differentiating themselves and establishing their tribal identity. They do this by giving their group a name (crips, bloods, Latin kings, brown pride, etc.), a way to identify themselves through specific tribal identifiers in the form of gang signs, and even by adopting a gang color to brandish in the community that signals to the rest of the world their specific tribal identity – in this case, their tribal identity being their gang affiliation. Here is a situation where oppression, violence, intimidation, exploitation, and unnecessary deaths occur on a rampant scale in gang-ridden communities, however, because it generally entails individuals of the same race involved in these acts, it cannot be labeled racism. And yet, the end results are just as devastating: it causes fear, intimidation, exploitation, violence, and death. Even in a sea of inherent similarities as is oftentimes the case in these communities, we still find ways to set ourselves apart from one another and then manufacture strife against each other for these differences that were purposely contrived. We, as humans, have a penchant for differentiation. We also have a penchant for tribalism. We create and manufacture tribes where none existed before and engage in strife and conflict amongst those manufactured tribes. It seems as if it is inherent in our DNA. We are primed and poised to engage in tribalism and tribalistic behavior.

RESILIENCE OF
RACIST IDEOLOGY

s it surprising that racism still exists in our modern day society? In a sense, yes, and, in another sense, no. In one sense, it's not surprising because, at the root of racism is grouping behavior, tribalism, differentiation, and territorialism – behaviors which are imbedded within us since ancient times and which we carry within us to this day, whether we are aware of it or not. From our earliest days, it was necessary for us to group together for survival. It was also necessary to have ways to identify who belonged to the group via tribal marking and tribal identifiers of some sort. These identifiers then helped to differentiate between groups. We carry these primal tendencies within us today as they are imbedded within our evolutionary biology and we apply them in a modern-world context. We constantly engage in grouping behavior, we constantly engage in tribal marking and signaling, we constantly engage in differentiating behavior, and we constantly engage in territorialism. These are drivers that we carry within us that influence our attitudes and behavior in a group context.

In another sense, it is surprising that racism still exists because, in our modern societies, we no longer have a practical need to apply these anciently developed behaviors in our everyday lives. However, just because innately imbedded behaviors are no longer practical does it mean that they dissolve or go away. They still remain within us and will do so unto the foreseeable future, as do our other primal drivers and instincts that, from time to time, resurface when called upon under the necessary conditions.

If we look at racism in its originally defined form, it entails oppressing, discriminating, and otherwise wringing harm (physical, psychological, economic, sociological) upon others due to their race and ethnicity. As such, racism can occur anytime these factors are present. All that is needed for racism to occur is for a person of one race to engage in oppressive and discriminatory behavior towards another person specifically because of that person's race or ethnicity. This can happen between just two persons of differing races or ethnic backgrounds or between groups of differing backgrounds. In essence, it can occur anytime intentionally oppressive and discriminatory actions are carried out between two parties due to one party's race or ethnicity. Anytime. There exists a common misconception that racism is one directional and can only occur when a person of "white" heritage or descent carries out discriminatory and oppressive actions and behavior towards a person of color. The reality is that racism can occur amongst many different groups and can be committed by anyone regardless of his or her race or ethnic identity. One does not have to be white to engage in racism, nor is a person who is white exempt from being the target of racism. Contrary to conventional wisdom, people of color can actually engage in racism themselves. This has happened since the advent of early human history.

As a person of Mexican descent, I am keenly aware of the legacy of racism that has been carried out by my ancestors against peoples of indigenous descent as Mexico expanded its territory Northward during colonial times and the atrocities that were committed towards indigenous peoples living in those territories as a result. Sadly, this racist mentality persists. To this day, people of indigenous descent suffer discrimination and are perceived with less regard and often with derision than those of non-indigenous heritage in Mexican culture. The irony of ironies is that, at its core, the essence of being Mexican is the intersection of Spanish and indigenous peoples, the blending of the two groups, the two cultures, so to be Mexican means deriving from both European (Spanish) blood as well as indigenous blood resulting in a blending of both heritages. When a person of Mexican heritage engages in discriminatory behavior against a person of indigenous descent, it is akin to engaging in an act of self-inflicted repression as indigenous blood is an intrinsic part of Mexican heritage.

That racism exists is irrefutable. It has been an inexorable part of our American history since before the founding of the nation. For those who experience it on an ongoing basis, it is quite real and distressing. For those who have never experienced it, however, it's quite a foreign concept and, for some, difficult to accept. It is extremely difficult for someone who has never encountered racism to appreciate the myriad of ways that this can be carried out in the course of everyday interactions with people and institutions. It's very difficult for someone to put himself or herself in another person's shoes who experiences racism without entering that person's body and experience life in that person's skin on a daily basis throughout the course of a lifetime. We can certainly be empathetic in this regard, however, empathy cannot replace a person's lived experiences.

Racism is real and it can be carried out by anyone regardless of his or her race as long as one person is engaging in intentionally harmful behavior towards another person due to race or ethnicity. That racism exists in our modern-day society is a reality. However, not everything is racism. Not all negative interactions between people are racially motivated. Sometimes, people just don't like each other for a whole slew of other reasons besides race or ethnicity – such is the human condition. Anybody can be mean, demeaning, arrogant, condescending, abusive, or obnoxious because that is just who they are at their core – regardless of his or her race or ethnicity. And people can carry themselves this way in their interactions with other people regardless of the other person's race or ethnicity. When others respond accordingly to somebody with qualities such as these, they are responding to these qualities within that person, not his or her race. The sad truth of the matter is that we can engage in oppressive, discriminatory, and violent behavior towards others regardless of race. People can also engage in oppressive, discriminatory, damaging, and violent behavior towards people of their own race and the end results can be just as damaging (as previously cited, much discrimination and oppression takes place in countries where the population is racially homogeneous including countries throughout Asia, Latin America, the Middle East, and Africa). However, when such destructive actions and behaviors involve people of the same race, it does not fit our conventional definition of racism, especially institutional racism. Sometimes, we get trapped in our man-made constructs and definitions in spite of the outcomes.

The harsh reality is that, we, as humans, consistently find ways to differentiate ourselves from one another not only racially, but in a myriad of other ways. We can't help but discern and recognize differences amongst each other and engage in discriminatory, oppressive, and harmful behavior accordingly due to those differences – whether overtly or covertly. We have always done so and will continue to do so far into the future. It's in our DNA. Our turbulent human history is a testament to this proclivity.

Race is but one of the myriads of ways that we engage in oppression, violence, and discrimination towards others. As humans, we are poised, primed, and wired to notice differences amongst one another. Even when race is not a factor, we still find ways to differentiate amongst each other, whether it's differences in language, culture, religious identity, political ideologies, the color we wear (as in gang colors), etc. We constantly find other ways to draw distinctions and notice the differences between us.

It is a common practice for the idealists amongst us subscribe to the notion that, in our modern society, we are beyond race and seeing the racial differences between us but that would be inaccurate. It's a beautiful notion and very idealistic, but the realities of the observable interactions amongst people tell us otherwise. Trump's ascendency on the waves of a xenophobic tide proved this. Even in his failed attempt at re-election, the sheer number of people who voted for him proved that we are as divided as ever and that there are many people who espouse his rhetorical overtones of xenophobia, misogyny, nationalism, and divisiveness. His message resonated with a large number of the populace and created a following for him that continues unabated and survived his thwarted bid for re-election.

In one of the scenes of the original Jurassic Park, Jeff Goldblum's character makes it a point to emphasize to the park administrators that life cannot be contained. Presumably, the park administrators had taken all the precautions necessary to ensure that no dinosaurs procreated outside of their purview by only producing female dinosaurs at the park and they were confident in all of their internal control measures and mechanisms that they had implemented to prevent this from happening. However, upon learning about all of these measures, Jeff Goldblum's character was unconvinced. He believed that, in spite of all of the measures that had been put in place, someway, somehow, life always finds a way. And, indeed, that is exactly what happened. Life found a way, even in the midst of an all-female population of dinosaurs. Somehow, the dinosaurs started breeding on their own. I feel that this is the case with our human penchant for differentiation. Somehow, it always finds a way. We, as humans, always find a way to recognize the differences amongst each other and treat each other with less regard due to those differences. Whether it's race, religion, language, gender, political ideologies, socioeconomic status, educational status, sexual orientation, body identity, age, etc., there is always something that we find to differentiate ourselves from one another, consciously or subconsciously. We can't help it. It is ingrained within us.

RACISM AND OUR
PRIMAL TENDENCIES

That racism exists in our modern society is undeniable. This is evident by the numerous groups who tout and subscribe to racist rhetoric and racist ideologies and do so overtly and proudly. An interesting phenomenon occurred with the advent of the Obama administration whereby a rhetorical claim began to surface and circulate that contended that his being elected to the highest post in the land signified the end of racism in the United States. While certainly a watershed moment in our nation's history, his being elected president did not indicate the end of racism in America as we know it. Of course, for those who experience racism and discrimination on an ongoing basis, they knew better than to believe such claims. Indeed, the lamentable truth of racism's unabated existence was then confirmed and highlighted once again when the Trump administration won the White House on a platform laced with divisive rhetoric that included xenophobia, nationalism, isolationism, and disparaged people of color, women, those with disabilities, prisoners of war (as was the case with Senator McCain), etc.......an era in which we witnessed an ushering in of an emboldened climate of racist tenor and activity in our country. It was an indicator that racism and xenophobia was indeed alive and well in the United States. It was, in fact, not dead as many had declared. It had never died.

The fact that Donald Trump won the presidency campaigning on a platform laden with such divisive rhetoric that vilified so many groups of people is quite telling of the nature of the society in which we currently find ourselves. The arc of the path that we had been laying forth in this regard had been underway for a long time and ultimately led us to such an eventuality. We, as a nation, had been trending toward this eventual outcome for some time when it actually came to pass. All the necessary ingredients were already present in our culture when Donald Trump happened to come along at an opportune time for him to recognize the tenor of the times and mix the societal and political ingredients available to him in his favor to produce a win. It was a confluence of events for sure – the political climate was rife and, in Trump, we were presented with a presidential candidate that was wholly and unabashedly unconventional and unapologetic about his nationalism and "home team" views as well as his aversion towards those who did not fit his ideals of an America for "real" Americans – an idealized vision of an America of the past. It was a "perfect" blending of timing and personality.

It is quite easy to point to Trump and place blame on him for the course of events that transpired during his presidency. To be sure, a lot of responsibility lies on him and on his conduct and influence while president, however, his being elected president was not the impetus of a rash of these kind of sentiments. It wasn't causal, it was symptomatic. His presidency was a symptom of a much more convoluted narrative in our society. Trump himself did not create racism, or nationalism, or xenophobia in our country, the conditions for those kind of sentiments already existed when he took power. The conditions that led to him gaining power had been developing for a long time. Trump just happened to come along at the right time to take full advantage of these pre-existing societal conditions.

I do not believe that Trump's ascendency to the presidency generated a wave of new recruits into a racist fold, although some people seem to think so. People who already have racist beliefs do not need to have someone in the White House leading the way and lighting the path so that they can be racist too. People with these beliefs and inclinations do fine of their own accord without the need of a captain at the helm to tell them what to think or how to act and behave. Also, people who are not racist nor have racist inclinations all of a sudden decide to become racist just because a president displays what could be construed as racist and xenophobic tendencies and behaviors. These beliefs and attitudes were already latent in the psyche of the nation. What his being elected did do, however, is create a climate where such sentiments could be more boldly expressed. People felt emboldened to express their pre-existing views and opinions more freely regarding issues of race and xenophobia where these may have been shared and disseminated only in a limited fashion and only in certain circles before. The genius of Trump's rise to power and, ultimately, to the Presidency, is that he was able to assess the prevailing winds of xenophobia and tribalism that were already brewing in the hearts and minds of millions, stoke those fires with his targeted messaging, market himself as a champion for this cause, and transmute all of these elements into a movement that won him a massive following and, ultimately, the White House. Once elected to power, those who subscribed to these kinds of sentiments viewed it as a legitimization of their cause and their ideologies. It had the effect of legitimizing and galvanizing their support for him and his message. After that, the floodgates were open, so to speak, as we witnessed a significant rise in racist rhetoric and activity during the course of his tenure as president, ultimately culminating in an insurrectionist and seditious attack of the U.S. capital. People feel emboldened whenever one of their own ascends to power – for good or ill.

PART SIX:

THE HOME TEAM

INNATE SENSE OF OWNERSHIP

As a collective group of people, those who have longstanding roots in the formation and founding of the United States have been people of Caucasian descent and, more specifically, WASP (White, Anglo-Saxon, Protestant), the heritage of the majority of the original colonists. (By "founding," I am referring to the collective and concerted actions of the original colonies to come together to form a union and codifying the laws by which that union would be governed. Native Americans were of course the original founders and finders of the land now known as the United States).

People of Caucasian descent have been the predominant racial majority for the lot of time the US has been a nation. Even prior to the founding and codifying of the nation, they had laid claim to vast expanses of North America before it officially became an independent nation when they were just a colony of the British crown. And then, they laid claim once again when the colonies declared their independence from England and the occupied territory was officially founded as a sovereign nation. With the course of these events as a backdrop, many people of Caucasian descent today carry this legacy within the depths of their psyche (consciously and subconsciously) and the identity that comes with it as being the founders of this nation. With it also comes a commensurate ethos of being the original and rightful owners thereof (a view that is both overt and covert). As such, there is an innate sense of ownership of these United Sates that stems from this conscious and subconscious perspective due to their direct antecedents having laid original "official" claim to it (a generational legacy of sorts). This is a legacy that casts a pall over the course of events stemming from the founding of the nation to the present day (asserted over time by such notions as Manifest Destiny, slavery, the Homestead Act of 1862, Jim Crow laws, segregation, etc.) and influences how subscribers of this notion carry themselves in their interactions with those who fall outside of this paradigm.

From the perspective of those who subscribe and embrace this mentality and carry it within them, this country is their land and, as such, they view themselves not only as the owners of these United States, but also as the stewards and caretakers of this nation and the protectors and defenders thereof (as would be the case for any of us who claim a stake in anything that we would consider as belonging to us). With claiming of a specific territory comes the marking of that territory as is the common behavior when a territory comes under the purview of a specific entity. It is marked through use of the various marking tools previously mentioned including borders, flags, seals, symbols, etc. And with the claiming and marking comes the defending of the territory against intruders. These are all instinctive behaviors.

However, what constitutes an "intruder?" Who exactly are the intruders in this regard? In this context, the "intruders" are those peoples who fall outside of this origin story – outside of this paradigm of original founding and ownership of the nation – those whom the "original owners" and stewards of this land view as "invading" their territory (or presented a pre-existing threat to territorial claims as was the case with Native Americans) – those who did not have a part of the original ownership group nor are they descendants thereof – those who were not part of the official laying claim or founding of the nation and their descendants, which essentially means those that are not of Caucasian descent (and, for large part of early American history, it was specifically those who were not WASP), they are the intruders and invaders in their eyes. As such, when they engage in acts of intimidation, aggression, and violence against people whom they view as "intruders" and "invaders" of their territory, they are acting on their innermost instincts to defend their territory against intruders just as we observe in nature. Instincts are difficult to dismiss or overcome. They are, by their very nature, instinctual.

As I write this, the events of January 6th, 2021 are unfolding at the nation's capital where thousands of angry Trump supporters stormed the capital building and besieged it as the nation and the world watched with incredulity and horror. That something like this could occur in the nexus of the American seat of government where one would expect security would be unparalleled is incomprehensible and there is yet a lot of investigating that will be taking place to analyze and dissect it all. This not withstanding, as I witnessed the scenes being televised and broadcasted, I couldn't help but recognize the tribalistic behaviors being acted out before our very eyes. All of which was mobilized and catalyzed by a person who epitomized these behaviors. It was truly a remarkable scene in the worst sense. And yet, there it was before us – those who considered themselves by and large the "original owners" of this nation defending it against something they viewed as an existential threat to its future (an "unlawful" claiming of the seat of control of the nation via a stolen election.) They viewed themselves not as terrorists or insurgents, but rather as the true defenders of a nation they considered to be at risk of being lost to the intruders and their sympathizers. They yelled and screamed as much as they ransacked the capital and carried their tribal markers (including Confederate flags), a clear example of territorial marking and defending behavior. Behavior that is innate and driven by evolutionary biology.

HOME TEAM
SYNDROME

As humans, we have a predilection for aligning ourselves with the "home team" which is the essence of tribalism. This is yet another behavior in which we engage at both a micro level as well as a macro level. We side with and support the "home team" with a fealty that can range from cursory at one end of the spectrum to fierce, blind loyalty at the other end. At the micro level, that fealty most often starts, understandably so, with our family and then expands concentrically outward to include other groups. Those other groups could include our neighborhood, our alma mater, our employer, the city in which we live (including the actual literal teams that are based there), the state in which we live, and the country in which we live. We have a penchant to align and side ourselves with the home team and to support and root for "our own." Of course, this is a manifestation of primal behavior that would have been necessary for self-preservation.... of the self and of the group or tribe. The tribe would have natural expectations that an individual's fealty and loyalty would be for the tribe itself and not for any other tribe. This fealty would need to be unequivocal and unquestioned, especially when engaging in conflict with other tribes. If an individual's loyalty and fealty could not be counted upon, that would be detrimental for the tribe and would, in turn, be detrimental for the individual as he or she would most likely be swiftly disposed of in some way.

In our modern-world context, the question arises as to who is the home team and who exactly are those who would constitute "our own?" What does "our own" mean? Our own could mean our families and our home town teams, but it could also include other groups to which we have aligned ourselves, expressed allegiance to, and adopted as "our own" such as a political party, a religion, or an ideology. There exist any number of ideologies which one could espouse and the options are vast and varied. Often, the aligning of ourselves to our various groups and their respective ideologies doesn't happen in a silo as usually there is a confluence and inter-sectionality of these elements that lead us in a certain direction. A person can subscribe to several parallel ideologies concurrently and the combination of these separate elements contribute to the person's overall identity. When the combination of these elements attracts a large number of people, of followers, the resulting effect is the formation of a movement, for better or worse – a movement with noble intentions.....or nefarious ones.

In the process of this alignment and of rooting for "our own" (the home team), we also develop a disdain for those whom we view as an existential threat to "our own," to our "home team," our tribe and the ideological identity of that tribe. These we would consider as being our rivals and enemies as they not only do not belong to the home team, but actually represent an existential threat to the home team.

As I write this, the dissection and analysis is unfolding regarding the insurgency that took place on the US capital building on January 6th, 2021. Many commentators and analysts are comparing and contrasting the stark differences in the level of security and police response that took place between this event and the Black Lives Matters protests that also took place in Washington DC several months prior. The commentators are asking how such an insurrectionist uprising was allowed to unfold and get out of control with a seemingly very sparse police response (especially given the intelligence available) as compared to the BLM protests which contained a much more robust police and law enforcement presence and response including a multi-agency law enforcement contingency consisting of Border Patrol agents, the National Guard, and even Blackhawk military helicopters. These are valid and necessary questions to ask, of course. As I hear the commentary, I find it somewhat bemusing because, at its core, it's so exemplary of the home team syndrome. The protesters that ransacked the capital on January 6th were members of the home team, inspired and incited by one of their own (and not just any one of their own, but the actual big kahuna of their own in the president of the United States himself) whereas the BLM protests and the protesters that participated in them represented those who are not part of the "home team." They were led largely by people of color with an agenda that called for a stop to police brutality against African-Americans and, moreover, a call for more societal equity in general – essentially, to be treated equitably and fairly and not as second-class citizens (an agenda antithetical to the home team as it represents an existential threat to the home team if it is to retain power.) Those protests consisted of large proportions of people of color (the "intruders" and "invaders") calling for justice and more equal treatment towards people of color by those in the seat of power and authority. They represented the "opposing" side, the intruders, not the "home team."

The stark police response in both incidents was the epitome of how members of the home team are viewed and treated differently than those who are not part of that group and how, when a specific group is viewed as the rival faction, that group is treated with much less regard and much more disdain due to their representing an existential threat to the home team. At times, such a disparity is implicit, subconscious, or covert. In this specific instance, however, the disparity was blatantly obvious and explicit precisely because the home team in this case had one of their own in a position where his clout and authority allowed him to have an immense amount of influence on the situation and how the situation was executed and carried out.

PART SEVEN:

TRIBAL PATRIOTISM

FEAR V. DISDAIN

The Black Lives Matter movement was forged out of necessity. When so many incidents of police brutality occur against otherwise unsuspecting, often unarmed, African-Americans, something had to give. BLM was borne out of this tragic injustice. A question that arises out of the heart of this matter is "why?" Why is it that this reprehensible phenomenon takes place and why does it keep happening, even as I write this? It is a sad and tragic reality that has become incomprehensibly consistent in our American narrative.

In an effort to make sense of the nonsensical, we subscribe to certain rationale as to why this continues to take place in our society. We cite hate, systemic racism, and implicit bias as being contributing factors at the root of the matter. Certainly, these factors can contribute to such tragic outcomes. What, however, contributes to a person developing these destructive attitudes and beliefs that lead to such tragic outcomes in the first place? One suddenly doesn't just wake up one morning and declare oneself a racist, or a bigot, or xenophobe, etc. There are contributing factors at play that lead to the development of these beliefs which, in turn, then lead to acts of violence and hatred. The disturbing part in this is that we all carry the potential to engage in these kind of attitudes and beliefs towards others within us. It's hard-wired into our evolutionary code of behaviors. A latent operating system of sorts that is programed into our hard drive.

How does one become a xenophobe and a racist? I believe that we all have the capacity to engage in a spectrum of such attitudes and behaviors because we all share a common ancestral narrative. This has indeed been exemplified throughout our human history. Especially during times of war and conflict. Indeed, we engage in war primarily due to these imbedded evolutionary biological traits and behaviors. We engage in combat with those whom we view as different than us in some form or another – whether ideologically, socio-politically, religiously, etc. A tribe does not go to war against itself as that would be counterintuitive, it goes to war against those whom it views as different in some capacity or another (even in the case of the American Civil War, the two sides represented different ideologies and it was those different ideologies that reconfigured the American tribe into the disparate Union v. Confederate tribes). We go to war when we differ in some way or another. When we differ, we see those who differ from us as our enemies and our opponents. We view them as a threat to our tribe, especially when there are contested territories at stake (physical territories as well as ideological ones). We have an internal drive to vanquish our enemies and our opponents and reap the benefits and spoils thereof.

In addition to these, there are also other forces at play, factors that are deeply rooted in our anciently coded behaviors, in our DNA. One of those factors is having an aversion to that which we find different from us. An aversion that is first catalyzed by our penchant for differentiation and which then moves us to act on this aversion response in conscious and unconscious ways. It moves us to act individually and can also move us to act as a collective – as one group of people towards another. This is exemplified quite saliently throughout the course of American history as various different waves of migrant groups landed on the shores of this ever-developing nation – not to mention the intrinsic attitudes that the first European settlers held towards the Native American peoples that were already here. With each wave of newcomers, the disdain and scorn exhibited from the established throngs of colonists towards the new arrivals highlights this point. Whether it was a wave of settlers from Sweden and other Scandinavian countries, a wave of workers from China brought to build the transcontinental railroad, a wave of immigrants fleeing famine-stricken Ireland, a wave of individuals of Italian descent, or immigrants from Eastern-block countries escaping violence and war, they all faced a harsh and rude awakening as they had to endure societal and systemic prejudice, disdain, and scorn from those who were already here – from the "home team," as it were. It's a story as old as human history itself.

We now think of these disparate groups as one conglomeration of "white" people and attribute the labels of white privilege and favoritism to persons deriving from these various heritages, but it wasn't always that way. With each new wave of immigrants and the new attributes and customs they brought with them, there was a commensurate wave of scorn and disdain from the "locals" towards the new arrivals as these new arrivals were seen and treated as outsiders, even in spite of the color of their skin. Although considered white by today's standards, they were still different in the eyes of those who were already here – by those who could claim "home team" status and long-standing roots in this country, which meant white, Anglo-Saxon, and Protestant. And they treated these "outsiders" accordingly. There exists a long history in our American narrative of mistreatment of peoples with each new diasporal wave due to their being of differing religions, speaking a different language, having different customs and traditions, different cultural practices, etc. With each new wave of people, a new way of engaging in prejudice and discrimination arose. Tribal behaviors indeed. We have a latent aversion for those whom we find different than us as part of our evolutionary biology, it just so happens that skin color is one of those differences that is very discernable and apparent and is a ready-made reason to discriminate against someone – a default pretext of sorts.

We come equipped with this penchant for aversion as standard operating equipment. When we become aware of this latent proclivity, however, we can then act with intention to overcome it. Of course, this is easier said than done as many of us live our lives without this recognition or awareness of how we developed these evolutionary behaviors and how they are imbedded deep within. However, if we are to make strides in these inherently difficult areas, we must become aware of this proclivity that we carry inside all of us so that we can face it and subjugate it if we want to be the accepting people that we aspire to be – as individuals as well as collectively as a group.

INSTINCTUAL PATRIOTISM

Since its founding, those who consider themselves as the "home team" have been the ones in charge of this nation. It has been so for centuries now. They've essentially called the shots, they've been the ones in power, they've been the predominant racial majority throughout the lot of that time. Throughout this span of time, those who subscribe to this mindset have regarded themselves as the rightful owners and the stewards of this grand experiment known as the United States of America and have taken it upon themselves to protect it against enemies and intruders, foreign and domestic. We, as humans, carry this instinctual penchant for guarding and protecting that which we claim as "our own," as "rightfully ours." This is a behavior that is universal and not exclusively attributable to people of any one ethnicity or race so it is not shocking or immensely revelatory that this has been the case in the context of these United States. We all practice this behavior and engage in it at a micro-level as well as at a macro level. We practice this behavior when we protect and guard our toys as children, when we protect and guard our families, when we protect and guard our homes, and when we engage in protecting and guarding our respective countries. Of course, when it pertains to guarding and protecting our countries, it isn't labeled as "instinctual protective behavior." It is regarded as patriotism. It's purely semantics, but the motives and the intended end results are all the same. Patriotism at its essence is the notion of guarding and protecting that which we consider "our own" in the context of a nation and doing so with, at times, unparalleled levels of loyalty and fealty even to the point of self-sacrifice which, in and of itself, is a supreme act of nobility and valor and must be regarded as such.

Seeing themselves as the founders and rightful owners, people of Caucasian descent who subscribe to this notion of "rightful ownership" also regard themselves as the stewards of this land, and the defenders thereof. This is at the core of patriotism and being a true patriot – defending, protecting, and sacrificing for the sake of country. Because of this, patriotism is bestowed with an immense amount of importance and one of the highest attributes a citizen can exhibit. It makes the quality of being patriotic very important in this respect. We see and hear this label touted constantly including in its inverse form when applied to disparage those whom are viewed as being less than patriotic – as lacking in patriotism. What exactly is patriotism, though? What does it mean to be patriotic? Let us explore this further.

Patriotism, at its core, stems from tribalism, plain and simple. It encapsulates the various aspects of tribal behavior. Patriotism is fed by tribalism and tribalistic behavior and tendencies. It is trib-alism scaled and applied in the context of an entire nation. With it comes all the trappings of tribalistic behavior including territo-rialism, marking and signaling, iconography, and defending of a particular territorial claim (and its people) – even unto death. It is tribalism scaled to apply to an entire nation. It is all of these things and also the commensurate displays of loyalty to the tribe that come along with such behaviors. Patriotism is fealty and loyalty to a spe-cific nation group and all that the nation (the tribe) represents and subscribes to including the various ideologies that the macro group considers important. This fealty can be expressed in different ways and it is also manifested in various ways. The external expressions of this kind of fealty include the various signaling, marking, and iconographical tools that demonstrate where one's loyalties and feal-ties lie including flags and banners, garb and uniforms, anthems, seals, emblems, mottos, etc. The inner manifestation of this fealty includes the emotions, beliefs, and esteem that one foments towards the collective group (the nation) and what it represents. The latter (the intrinsic feelings and emotions) are constantly being reinforced by the former (the markers and iconography). Indeed, the stronger these feelings become, the greater the significance that is given to the external markers, so much so at times that the markers them-selves are bestowed with such gravitas that they become the embod-iment of patriotism themselves, such as the American flag, the U.S. Constitution, the National Anthem, etc. Hence, any perceived or actual show of disrespect or lack of regard exhibited towards one of these symbols becomes, by proxy, a disrespect or disregard for all that the symbol represents and the person or group exhibiting such behavior is quickly chastised and labeled as being unpatriotic, even if the person is not unpatriotic. In the eyes of those who regard this behavior as evidence of a lack of patriotism, the underlying reasoning or motives for such behavior is inconsequential. The behavior itself suffices to apportion the unpatriotic label accordingly. The case of Colin Kaepernick is a perfect example of this phenomenon where his bringing attention to a systemic injustice in society by taking a knee during the National Anthem was seen as betrayal to the nation – a nation that he was trying to improve through a call to action by this specific gesture.

As patriotism is, at its core, instinctual tribal behavior, it is something that is within all of us and we all engage in this behavior across many cultures, across many nations, and across many contexts in some fashion or another. The universality of this behavior is evident in the way that individuals the world over are invariably loyal and patriotic towards "their own." This includes their own country, their own nation, their own culture, their own people, their own iconography – essentially, all the trappings that "their own" represents and holds dear. The universality of this behavior and its expressions of fealty and loyalty are conveniently evident whenever occasions involving a congregation of many nations takes place such as the Olympics or the World Cup (it is also evident during times of war). These events offer a convenient glimpse into tribalism and tribalistic behavior in one convenient aggregate, in one fell swoop, so to speak. These international events are laden with nationalistic and patriotic exhibitions of behavior as nations vie for superiority. The flags, colors, anthems, mottos, etc. of each respective nation represented at these events are exhibited in their full splendor as countries compete for glory through physical contests and the athletic achievements of its respective citizen-athlete representatives. It's a contest for superiority via the auspices of organized athletic competition that brings glory to the contestants and also to their respective nations as a whole. These events offer opportunities to fan the flames of patriotism for the respective countries represented. In this context, it is very normal for us to root for "our own" so that, through the success and achievements of "our" athletes, our own tribe (our nation) can be elevated in status and superiority. In the case of war amongst nations, these sentiments are imbued with a much higher level of gravity and consequence and the outcomes are much more literal as nations engage in actual battle for superiority via the execution of military force and military might against each other and the outcomes are much more consequential.

PROVINCIAL PATRIOTISM

This penchant for patriotism occurs across nations, but it is also evident at a regional scale within a country's own borders as certain regions within a country and the individuals who dwell within those regions adopt a regional form of patriotism in addition to or even in spite of a national patriotism. Such is the case, for example, in areas such as Catalonia in Spain, the area of Northern Ireland in Ireland, nation-states such as Taiwan in China, Quebec in Canada, and various other regions of the world. We can also see a regional form of patriotism here in the United States particularly when it pertains to those who claim the South and Southern heritage as being a sociological and ideological tenet that, for those who subscribe to it, holds immense significance and importance for them. For those who subscribe to this particular regional kind of patriotism, they regard it as a part of their heritage and an intrinsic part of their culture and cultural identity – for themselves and their families. This is especially true if their families have a longstanding history of being connected to and have long-standing ties to the region considered "the South." As such, they hold on to those symbols, artifacts, and signaling markers that are representative of that Southern culture and Southern heritage as any other group of people would do for their own respective culture and heritage. In doing so, they also engage in a commensurate defending of that culture and the iconography that is representative of that culture (such as the confederate flag, historical landmarks, historical names, statues of historical figures, etc.) as would be expected when viewed through the lens of instinctual tribal behavior – in this case manifested as regional patriotism.

From an outsider's point of view, when individuals and families engage in this protective behavior of their Southern culture and heritage, the default perspective is to see that behavior solely as a nefarious desire to hold on to a dark part of American history that denigrated, oppressed, and brutalized African-Americans. While this may be true for some individuals who embrace this particular sort of regional patriotism, a blanket statement cannot be applied to all such individuals. Some are simply reacting instinctually to any such attack against something that has been part of their heritage for generations. They are reacting to something that is being attacked that has been an intrinsic part of their identity for as long as they can remember. Their reactive response is, in essence, the instinctual reaction or instinctual tendencies for any of us whose culture and heritage were under attack – even if that cultural heritage had negative undertones.

We all carry an instinct to become defensive and protective of that which we hold dear such as our families, our community, our alma maters, our nation, our respective culture and our respective heritages and engage in defensive and protective behavior if we feel these are under attack or threatened, rightly or wrongly. If we view this behavior through the lens of evolutionary biology and instinctual behavior, it makes perfect sense. It doesn't diminish the negative nature that these symbols represent for others, but it makes more sense as to why people embrace and defend these even to this day in spite of their negative connotations. In the eyes of those who embrace these sentiments and attitudes of attachment towards this heritage and its iconography, these do not represent an outdated, oppressive history, they represent their heritage, a living heritage, a heritage that they hold dear and which is a part of their individual and familial identity. To eradicate and attack these symbols takes on the equivalence of attacking their cultural identity and, by proxy, becomes an attack on their person and family. The resulting reactive responses are not surprising – when one's culture and heritage are under attack as it is in their eyes, the resulting backlash is predictable. We see the reactive behavior to this specific phenomenon widely in the US as historical artifacts are questioned and attacked and, at times, destroyed, but especially in those Southern states where a wave of artifacts and iconography representative of the oppressive South has come under threat of being removed, eradicated, and replaced ("cancelled"). The resulting outcomes are not an embracing of new symbolism or a passive acceptance of the destruction of old symbolism. It's quite the opposite. The systematic process or eradicating these symbols has produced rocket fuel for a movement that was already in motion. It has produced an attitude of galvanized defiance against the tide bent on the erasure of negative symbolism and history. Trump tapped into this fervent wave with machiavellian deftness. In him, those who viewed their micro-heritage being attacked via the auspices of political correctness as well as those who held a romanticized notion of their America slipping away and being erased had a champion in Trump. His rhetoric of harkening to a romanticized notion of an idealized America of the past as well as his dismissive attitude regarding calls to action from progressive groups fighting for a more politically sensitive environment made him the perfect stalwart for their cause and helped to carry him into the White House where he became the embodiment of this ideology during his tenure and where he evoked this attitude unabashedly.

RELATIVITY OF PATRIOTISM

When patriotism is viewed through the lens of unwavering loyalty and fealty to a nation, those who would question or critique it and the representative government thereof for questionable acts, motives, and actions are quickly labeled as unpatriotic and even as traitors. In such a climate, to critique, question, or criticize the actions of the representative government is tantamount to an act of betrayal towards the nation which the government represents and, moreover, towards its people. In the eyes of many, the adopted groupthink attitude is to support one's country, to support one's nation and its actions and motives unwaveringly – "America, love it or leave it!"

It is extremely difficult to be an independent thinker or critical thinker in an environment where one's loyalty to country is readily questioned and denounced for any sort of critique or observation that goes against the grain of what is conventionally accepted – no matter how valid those observations and criticisms may be. This has been especially true during times of conflict and war against other nations (the Vietnam War era and the detractors thereof were the epitomes of this premise). Over time, however, this penchant for slinging the "unpatriotic" epithet has become more and more commonplace in correlation with the increasingly polarized and divisive political climate that we have cultivated. In our current climate, terms such as liberal and conservative have been rebranded and their meanings reconfigured by the opposing side so as to make them essentially pejoratives. As such, their meanings have been twisted so as to represent the worst possible configuration of the word by the opposing side to a level where they have become the modern-day equivalents of communism v. fascism (although we don't use those terms exactly, instead we use the descriptors: the "radical left" and the "radical right"). To go along with these pejoratives, the "unpatriotic" label is also thrown in there for good measure and for added negative effect. The intent of assigning this label, of course, is to tear down and dehumanize the "other" side as much as possible so that those belonging or subscribing to the opposing ideology are viewed through an ever clouded and distorted negative lens, which, in essence, has the effect of widening the gap of divisiveness ever more.

Patriotism and questioning another person's level of patriotism has become part and parcel of today's political rhetoric. Nobody wants to be labeled unpatriotic, yet many are ready to sling this label and ascribe it to another person who has differing views than they do. To toss around the unpatriotic label and to question another person's patriotism has become an American political sport of sorts and those who sling it best gain the approval and adulation of their respective party.

What exactly does it mean to be patriotic, though? Because being patriotic means different things to different people, it inevitably causes differences of opinion amongst the masses. And these differing views of patriotism lead to widening the schisms in our society. Does patriotism mean that one supports and follows the government's policies with utter fealty and devotion (with blind loyalty)? For some people, this is what patriotism means to them – support of country no matter what. For others, patriotism ultimately means being willing to lay down one's life for his or her country. This is unquestionably noble, of course, however, if one is to lay down one's life as the ultimate act of patriotism in the course of war or conflict against another nation, that means that, commensurately, there is a person on the opposing side who is also willing to do the same for their country – who is also willing to lay down his or her life for the cause being touted by the nation that he or she represents – and so they too are being the ultimate patriots for their respective side. In essence, both individuals are being patriotic – each one for his or her respective side. Both are being the ultimate patriots. However, we don't normally view it this way. We have a tendency to view only those who represent "our own," those who are on "our side," as being patriotic and we view the ones on the opposing side – the "other side" – as being something akin to evil monsters incapable of such noble notions such as patriotism (such as the Viet Cong during the Vietnam War and the Japanese and Germans during World War II). We view patriotism through the distorted lens of our tribalistic tendencies.

And what happens when a person is willing to lay down one's life for his or her country in battle against other individuals of the same country such as occurs in civil war? Who is deemed patriotic then at that point? The rebel side or the incumbent government side? Were the Confederate soldiers being patriotic towards their side and unpatriotic towards the Union? Was patriotism reserved only for their cause when they were fighting against the Union Army? Or were the Union soldiers that were fighting to keep the nation from breaking apart the ones that were being patriotic? Were the American colonists being patriotic when they were fighting the British Crown for independence? Or were those who objected to breaking apart from the Crown the ones who were being patriotic towards the British Crown? It all depends on one's perspective. Certainly the British Crown viewed the American colonists loyal to the Crown as patriotic. However, the American rebels viewed these same individuals as traitors to the American call for independence. And what if the revolution had not succeeded, those same supporters and leaders of the revolution would have been labeled as traitors to the Crown and most likely executed.

Were the individuals who ransacked the US Capitol on January 16, 2021 being patriotic? They certainly believed so. It was an uprising for something they felt was necessary to right a wrong for their country. They certainly viewed themselves as being patriotic and exhibited all the trappings and iconography to illustrate this to the world as they carried flags, signs, and symbols indicating as much in the course of their siege. They were prepared to engage in extreme actions and go to extreme lengths for their cause, which they deemed necessary to save the country – "their" country – from being governed in a way they deemed was illegitimate (via a stolen election).

When uprisings take place to right a wrong (justified or not), we tend to view these uprisings through different lenses depending on which side of the political spectrum we fall under. One person's act of patriotism is another person's act of riotist insurgency or hooliganism. Many people on the right side of the political spectrum, including the sitting president at the time, viewed the attack on the US capitol as a necessary act to rectify a perceived miscarriage of justice in the claim that the election had been stolen. In this way, this act was viewed as an act of patriotism in an attempt to rectify that particular wrong, and, yet, when similar acts are carried out to right wrongs caused by discriminatory policies against people of color, those insurgencies are typically regarded and labeled as anything but patriotic by those same people, such as the taking over of the state capitol in Oregon or the protests against police brutality in the wake of the death of George Floyd at the hands of police. Instead, these were labeled as anti-government mobs and riots even if the intended ends are similar (to right wrongs – real or perceived – for the betterment of a nation and its people). It's interesting how the lens through which we view the world skews our perspectives in one direction or another based on our political leanings.

PART EIGHT:

OUR COLLECTIVIST TENDENCIES

INERTIA OF POWER
AND CONTROL

During the course of events leading to the American Revolution, much discourse, machinations, and plotting took place amongst the colonists centered around the myriad of perceived injustices that were being dispensed by the British Crown and their monarch, King George III. The colonists, after numerous attempts to redress and rectify these injustices, reached the point of conclusion that there was no other viable recourse but to cut all ties and become independent from the Crown and embarked on the path towards that goal which included numerous acts of defiance, violence, and ultimately, insurrection in the form of revolution.

In our modern-day context, when we hear or witness organized acts of violence, defiance, insurrection, and rebellion on behalf of any group, we have the automatic tendency to regard the persons involved in these acts as a gang of miscreants, an impetuous mob, a band of misfits, etc. – essentially as lacking in any form of prudence or redeemable qualities – as being up to no good. Those who engage in such acts are typically disenchanted with the order of things and are seeking change of some sort – a change for which they are willing to rise up and fight for – as was the case with the American Revolutionaries. The American Revolutionaries were seeking change, plain and simple, and were willing to fight for it – to die in the process if necessary.

Change can be very disruptive, at times necessarily so. Some changes such as the American independence from Britain require acts of defiance and uprising to bring them about. In our modern perspective of these change agents, we do no regard the American Revolutionaries as anything but brave and noble men and women willing to fight the powers that be – the oppressors – the despotic British Crown. We regard them as the ultimate patriots. However, they were indeed insurrectionists. They were calling for a change to the status quo, the order of things at the time. In order to bring those changes about, insurrection and rebellion was necessary via the auspices of a revolution. In so doing, they were the embodiment of progressiveness and the direct opposite of conservatism. Conservatism subscribes to the notion of preserving and conserving the order of things. The American Revolutionaries were intent on flipping the order of things on its head. They sought a new way – a new form of government, a new nation, a new start. Those who espouse conservatism and conservative values today must exercise judiciousness and be very wary of invoking the founders of the nation, the

American Revolutionaries, as a reflection of the conservative values of today for the American revolutionaries were all about change and new ways of doing things, not conservatism. Change is the antithesis of conservatism. Someone who espouses conservatism and conservative, traditionalist values is distrustful and trepidatious of change. Those in power, those in control, those who hold the societal reins resist change as they do not want to relinquish the power, the control, the reins that they have held and enjoyed for so long as was the case with the British Crown. Maintaining and conserving the status quo ensures a continued level of power and control and a prolonged tenure of being at the helm. Change can upend that.

Those who are in a position of power and control do not concede that power or give up their control easily or readily. In fact, quite often, they will go to extreme lengths to preserve and maintain control for as long as possible (we have witnessed this throughout history via oligarchical and imperialist monarchies prior to the advent of democratic republics and, in more modern history, via authoritarian regimes and dictatorships such as was the case with Stalin, Lenin, Mao, Francisco Franco and in more recent times with Fidel Castro's tenure of being at the Cuban helm of power, Pinochet in Chile, Deterte in Africa, and many others, all of whom were in power for a protracted number of years through systematic state-sponsored acts of oppression, intimidation, and violence against their critics and detractors). In these instances, preserving the order of things benefited them as it ensured their continuance of being in power and control. As a result, it often takes a herculean effort, often in the form of revolution, to bring about the change that is necessary. This was the case during the American Revolution. The British Crown did not, by any means, give in easily to the American colonists' demands for independence and a lot of lost lives and bloodshed ensued as a result. It came at a huge cost, precisely because those in power and control did not want to relinquish the power and control they held (we even witnessed a form of this unwillingness to concede power phenomenon in our most recent presidential election!).

In today's context, those in power also do not want to give up that power and control that they currently hold and have enjoyed for generations. We are in the midst of that systemic socio-political transition of power right now and have been for some time (incremental as it might be) as evidenced via the gains in societal footholds by the traditionally disenfranchised of this country including women, people of color, people of differing gender identities, differing religious faiths, etc.

Those who are in power, those who are in control, typically do not relinquish control without a fight. This is typical and observable across species. In the animal kingdom, the dominant alpha animal of any group does not relinquish control of a territory or a herd against a competitor without a fight. When a change in power and control happens, it happens by force. Throughout the course of our American history, we have seen a similar phenomenon play out consistently on various occasions and circumstances. Independence from Britain was won by force, slavery was ended by force, Jim Crow was upended through many trials, tribulations, and force, women's suffrage was a long-fought battle, civil rights were likewise obtained through violence and bloodshed, as was school desegregation, etc. All of these changes have come about through hard-fought battles, both literal and metaphorical in the streets and in the court system. These kinds of systemic changes are not easily given or granted nor are they easily attained. We continue the battles even today as the BLM movement, #MeToo movement, cancel culture, etc. have shown us. And the resistance to these changes continues as well.

Oftentimes, change of the systemic and institutional kind produce and foment bitterness and resentment that can lead to hatred amongst those who oppose such change. I am reminded of the disturbing images that were captured and which are now iconic in the aftermath of the Brown v. Board of Education Supreme Court decision which declared "separate but equal" education as unconstitutional. In the tumultuous aftermath of this ruling, much opposition transpired against its implementation. An iconic image was captured in the vortex of this firestorm in which, amidst a sea of white individuals lined up leading to the schoolhouse in Little Rock, Arkansas being surveyed by Federal troops, angry throngs protested the group of nine African-American students being escorted to the school building which signified the end of school segregation. A woman in the crowd, livid with rage at the scene before her, took it upon herself to show her disdain by hurling vicious epithets at one of the girls as she walked along, her vitriolic expression of rage captured forever on film. Change, especially systemic and institutional change, is oftentimes extremely difficult to bring about, to enact, to implement. Oftentimes, it comes at a great cost. Oftentimes, it is accompanied by invidiousness, hatred, and resentment. Sometimes, it takes centuries for change to gain traction and to take hold. It is not always a straight line, nor does it always move in a forward motion. Sometimes, it goes backward in response to reactionary backlash.

ZERO-SUM GAME

Given that this racial socio-political dynamic exists in our nation, we are always trying to make sense of it. We analyze it, we dissect it, we organize seminars and workshops around it, we have panel discussions about it, we design curricula and classes around it, all in an attempt to increase our awareness, reduce its prevalence, and, ultimately, to eradicate it. We do this in response to and, sadly, even as incidents of racial violence continue to take place around us in communities all across the nation (and around the world). The reality is that one cannot undo deeply imbedded instincts and instinctual drivers that contribute to behavior that can be construed as racist, no matter how many classes or workshops a person participates in. Instincts are hard-wired. One can learn to suppress acting on an instinct, but that doesn't mean that the instinct goes away. It is still there. Instincts can lie latent, dormant, but not erased which means that, given the right set of circumstances, these instincts can become activated and acted upon. I don't make this contention lightly as, being an idealist myself, I would like to believe that racism and bigotry could indeed be eradicated. I would like to envision a world where humanity could live in harmony with one other regardless of our inherent differences. However, our collective pattern of behavior as a species over millennia dictates otherwise.

We, as modern humans, have been on this earth for a long time (relative to our individual life spans), approximately 200,000 years. Within that span of time, we have been on earth long enough to make monumental advancements and amazing progress in a myriad of arenas: the development of civilizations, development of language, development of mathematics, innumerable scientific and medical discoveries and advancements, development of technology, architectural and engineering marvels, the list goes on and on......we have transformed the world in which we live for our own purposes and for our own benefit in ways that are astounding – unlike any other organism in the earth's history spanning billions of years. And yet, even with all of these achievements, discoveries, and advancements, this primal set of behaviors remains within us. It is ubiquitous and present in us as humans no matter what part of the globe we examine. In all corners of the earth, there is injustice and oppression taking place right now due to some sort of inherent differences and differentiation between groups of people, whether physical or ideological. We have always done this from our earliest days throughout human history. This tendency has not been shed or discarded. Even now in our most advanced societies (of which the United States is arguably at the forefront), this behavior continues unabated. And it will continue because it is imbedded deep within us. It is in our DNA.

We have always found a way to be at odds with each other due to some difference that we recognize in others whether it be a physically manifested difference such as skin color and gender, or an ideological difference including religion, political ideologies, and even economic ideologies. We find a way to recognize differences, to let those differences divide and separate us, and then to become contentious towards one another due to those differences as we try to quell the differences which we view as threatening. We do this even as new differences surface in the form of new ideologies, new ideas, and new ways thinking.

Some people rightly point out that it is mutually beneficial if we all do our best to uplift everybody by ensuring that everybody has the same rights, same opportunities, same access to resources, and is treated equally as this will help us to prosper as a collective people, as a nation, as a world. While that is a beautiful notion, it just will not come to pass so long as there are those who don't espouse this goal and don't care about manifesting this concept – those who do not want this to come to pass because of their inner tribal tendencies and the fear of loss of control and power – of being gradually supplanted. Just like we would not help an intruder who came into a home and tried to gain a foothold, those who regard themselves as the original owners of this nation do not want the "intruders" to prosper. In fact, quite the opposite. Those who are regarded as the intruders are seen as a threat, the rival enemy and, instinctually, one does not help one's enemy to prosper lest the enemy gains ever more power, stature, and control. That would be counterintuitive to our tribal instinctual behaviors and our drive for self-preservation. It goes against our basic instincts to help and uplift those whom we consider an existential threat to us and our way of life (whether the threat is real or imagined) lest they gain power and supplant us. This line of thinking is at the essence of the new form of conservatism, especially that which is touted by Donald Trump and his followers.

In his version of conservatism, those who espouse conservative values inherently want to conserve the ideologies, attitudes, beliefs, and customs that they regard as the essence of an America that they regard as the "true" and proper vision of America – an America of the past. To impose changes to this model of America is corrosive to the idealized model of America that they hold dear. In order to prevent this from happening, they will resist and fight against those ideas, ideologies, and movements that can erode this traditionalist version of America and the players who tout these – namely those representing the opposing side – those who want to enact change and implement policies that challenge these neo-conservative ideologies – those on the left side of the political spectrum, namely, liberals and progressives.

Commensurately, those on the other side of the spectrum espouse a vision of America as one which must cast off outdated, traditionalist ideologies they consider archaic if the nation is to evolve into one that is inclusive of all sectors of society. This is a notion that is terrifying and quite disturbing towards those on the conservative side for they value tradition and constancy, not change. Change can be a very frightening and disconcerting phenomenon for many of us. We have a tendency to find comfort in constancy. Change is the opposite of that – ideological change even more so.

So we are left with two dichotomies – two diametrically opposed approaches towards a similar end goal – that of ensuring this, the place we call home, is the best country that it can possibly be. The end goal may be the same, but the vision of the finished product is quite different from the respective vantage points of both camps. Which way is right and which way is wrong? That depends on which vantage point one utilizes to view the matter. Certainly, those on the conservative side view the liberal, progressive approach as being misguided and wrong whereas those on the liberal, progressive side view the conservative approach similarly flawed and misguided. This leads to discord, which leads to divisiveness and the commensurate discrediting of the opposing sides to make them seem incompetent and delusional, as well as a systemic smear and dehumanization campaign to go along with it. For those who subscribe to either of these views, their attitudes towards them become ever more entrenched and ossified by the attacks of the opposing side as well as the constant assurances extolled from the echo-chambers of their own partisan media outlets and personality figures in the guise of confirmation bias. It is a battle of wills as well as a battle to win over the hearts and minds of the populace – a people divided. Divided by tribalistic tendencies.

COLLECTIVISM AND MOB MENTALITY

As humans, we have great capacities. We have the capacity to act of our own accord and of our own agency – to go at it alone. However, we are also wired to be social creatures and to engage with others as a group. We have an inner drive that compels us to do this. In a group, we become a component of a greater whole and it produces within us feelings of great satisfaction to be a part of something that is bigger and greater than ourselves – to be able to be part of a team and to work towards a collective goal. Any of us who have experienced collaborative teamwork in this context whether through sports, in a work setting, a volunteer opportunity, emergency response and crisis intervention, etc. know full well the great and rewarding aspect and the feeling of satisfaction one experiences from working on something together. It feels great. That is because it nurtures our primal need to belong as social creatures and also feeds that inner drive to collaborate as a group, as a collective.

This innate drive to work together for a common purpose, a common goal can also yield awful outcomes, however, when that overarching goal is a nefarious one. When the common goal is the oppression, eradication, and evisceration of a peoples, it represents the dark side of this collaborative aspect of our innate instinctual behaviors. Working collaboratively, we have a great capacity for good, however, the potential also exists to work collaboratively for harm.

When, as an individual, we feel threatened, we innately revert to the primal portion of our brain, the limbic system, via a fight or flight mode. We default to a primal mode of operating and act according to that default operational mode within us – it takes over. When we feel threatened as a group, we, collectively revert to a fight or flight mode and act accordingly from a primal default mode – only this time as a collective unit – a concerted effort. We can engage in a mob mentality of sorts and will do and say things for the benefit of the greater whole. We, at various points in time, will abdicate our individualism for collectivism to advance the cause, the goals, the ideologies of the larger, collective group to whom we belong and to whom we feel a deep sense of loyalty (we engage in denial and sacrifice of the self for the benefit of the whole). We do this often, whether it's in the context of a relationship, a family, a team, an employer, a faith community, or a nation. There exist many instances when we put our own individual interests aside for the sake and benefit of the group – the greater good as it is oftentimes referred. We, in a sense, lose ourselves in the identity of the larger group, the collective. We become a cog, a component of the machinery that is the greater group – that is the essence of collectivism and collectivist ideology. We become a single-minded organism of sorts. This phenomenon occurs frequently. It occurs amongst our micro-groups on a small scale and it also occurs amongst our macro groups, such as a nation, on a large scale. When, at a macro-scale, this collectivist mentality is applied towards the eradication of particular groups of people as a means to "protect" the greater group (our tribe) and preserve and defend its overarching goals, values, and ideologies, the outcomes are tragic.

That this spirit remains in the hearts of many is a testament to the staying power of these human tendencies and inclinations. Many groups abound ubiquitously around the globe who espouse these axioms and ideologies. It is a testament that we, as humans, have a penchant and a proclivity for this kind of collectivist behavior – a group mentality on a large scale.

HARSH REALIZATIONS

One of the amazing functions that we, as humans, can engage in is an ability to collaborate and work together as a cohesive unit for a common purpose or goal. This capacity for collaboration has enabled us to develop agriculture, build communities, to found nations, to develop civilizations. It has allowed us to build amazing structures, to build cities, to engage in seemingly impossible collaborative feats of civil engineering as well as the production of goods that we all benefit from. It has enabled us to build nations and to bring down despotic governments when necessary. It has allowed us to organize and carry out revolutions – intellectual revolutions as well as political ones – and to reconstruct governments once again; to organize movements for the greater good and betterment of society and to accomplish amazing feats of scientific, technological, and medical discoveries and ingenuity. By working together, sharing resources (intellectual, material, and technological), we have been able to accomplish amazing things and continue to do so in this way. This trajectory has led us to our current place in time where we have immeasurable systems in place to help us function as a modern civilization. These, of course, have not come without cost and consequences for our endeavors in the form of pollution of our water, air, and soil and the precipitated extinction of many species. However, the same cooperative efforts that create these collateral negative by-products is the same type of collaboration that can help us address and ameliorate them. We are able to come together and collaborate for a common goal or purpose. Oftentimes, that purpose can move humanity forward. At times, however, it can set us back.

There are many times throughout the course of human history where we, as a collective group of people, have engaged in gross atrocities against another group of people. Unfortunately, the examples abound when we did not see eye to eye with others; when our differences were too much to tolerate; when our faiths, ideologies, territorial claims were more than could be mediated. Too often, we have allowed our intrinsic differences to be the catalyst for horrible violence against others of large-scale proportions.

Our grouping instinct has allowed us to navigate our world in a way that enabled us to survive and thrive for eons. Groups, tribes, teams, communities, work well together when the individual members, the disparate components, if you will, are in concert and alignment with the overarching mission and vision of the whole – when there is a shared goal and a common sense of purpose amongst all who comprise a particular group. We crave this sense of teamwork, of belonging to and being part of a collective enterprise, and of working towards a common goal as part of our inner drive and inclinations as social creatures. The common purpose or goal, however, is not always noble. It can be nefarious and destructive.

Many of us reading this book (although not all) view human suffering, human atrocities, and genocide with abject horror. We have a difficult time fathoming how such events occur and take place – how, as a collective group of people working together, we, as humans, could engage in the act of purposely eradicating (or attempting to eradicate) another group of people. It is unfathomable and unthinkable. However, it is important to understand that, whenever these events have transpired, the persons involved in carrying out and supporting these acts have been people not unlike you and I – made of the same organic biological composition, innate tendencies, emotions, intelligence, and inherent internal wiring such as you and I. They were modern humans just like we are, essentially made of the same stuff in our inherent composition.

This is a harsh realization to be sure. We do not perceive ourselves as capable of the atrocities of our forebears and, yet, as a species, we continue to engage in these acts even in modern times for it was our forebears that directly or indirectly engaged in these acts not so long ago – in 1940s Germany, the Jim Crow South in the United States, The US during Westward Expansion, the US during slavery. It was our forebears, our forefathers who did these things. We could have very well done the same thing or been party to these phenomena were we to have been alive and present during those specific time frames. Some reading this book in fact were alive and present when some of these events took place. With the benefit of our modern-day vantage point, we like to think that we are above this kind of behavior and, yet, we continue to engage and do these acts as humans. We like to think that we would not, could not possibly carry out these kinds of unspeakable acts. It is easier "thought" than done, however. When in the face of these realities, how do we know how we would really act? Are we capable of going against the grain of the collective? Against the tribe? Against the tide of the wave in which we are in? That is what transpired in these cited examples. People such you and I engaged in these acts. We could very well have committed and been a part of these atrocities were we to have been alive and present whence these occurred and had been active members of these societies and the tribes who committed them. In spite of our good intentions, history has shown that we are quite prone to vilify and dehumanize those whom we view as different if those presenting differences represent an existential threat to us. Collectivism and mob mentality is real and we are much more impressionable than we recognize – as a people and as a nation. We witnessed this quite saliently in the way the events of January 6th, 2021 transpired from the conception to the execution thereof.

PART NINE:

COMING TO TERMS

COMING TO TERMS

While still a Jr. Senator from Illinois, former President Barak Obama gave his now famous speech at the 2004 Democratic National Convention that, essentially, launched his run for President. In it, he extolled the notion that "there is no white America, there is no black America, there is only the United States of America!" Of course, he was expressing that we, as Americans of all faiths, creeds, and color are one people. We are a nation comprised of individuals from a variety of different backgrounds, but we are one people nevertheless. It was a call to stop focusing on the things that make us different and look for the qualities that unite us – essentially that we are all Americans.

It is a noble and beautiful notion for sure. However, this is a notion that has eluded us as humans even after 6,000 years of modern civilization. After all this time, we continue to act and behave as if we are all from disparate groups – disparate tribes. We cannot erase millions of years of evolutionary biology. It is ingrained within us. As long as differences exist amongst us, we will treat one another with a certain level of suspicion, distrust, aversion, and hate due to those differences – consciously as well as subconsciously. We naturally gravitate and congregate with those who are most like us (racially, culturally, ideologically) and, as such, engage in the commensurate tribalistic behaviors that are corollaries of this grouping phenomenon. These we carry within us and we cannot change that. We have to contend with these tendencies and with those who embrace and espouse them to their fullest extent. As long as these tendencies and inclinations are within us as humans, there exists the potential for us to apply them in our interactions with others, consciously as well as subconsciously. Being aware of this reality helps us to be cognizant that we carry these innate tendencies within as part of our DNA. Once aware, we can then be better suited to rein these in and modulate them in our interactions with others and in our views and beliefs about others. We cannot control that of which we are not aware. By being aware of these, our inner tendencies, we are much better equipped to recognize them and to deal with them whenever they present themselves.

This is our reality. Our reality as humans with primal tendencies living in a modern world. We can postulate that we are above these innate tendencies and tribalistic behaviors – that we are evolved – that we are "woke." However, the annals of human history dictate otherwise as it is replete with the markers of atrocities and genocides that we have committed against each other over our tribalistic differences. And we continue to foment and engage in these even as I write this. Our innate primal instincts get the better of us more often than we are aware of or like to admit.

There is a danger in thinking and believing that we are above these inclinations because then we become susceptible to collectivism and collectivist thought which has the potential to lead us into dark paths as has happened so many times before. The reality is that these innate inclinations are imbedded within all of us. We ignore them and discount them at our peril.....and the peril of others.

We all have great capacities to influence our interactions with those around us – as individuals and as a collective. A great capacity for good as well as a great capacity for ill.